MELTZER IN SÃO PAULO

Working with Meltzer Series

Meltzer in Paris
edited by Jacques Touzé

Meltzer in Venice
edited by Maria Elena Petrilli, Hugo Màrquez,
and Mauro Rossetti

*Psychoanalytic Work with Children and
Adults: Meltzer in Barcelona*
edited by Donald Meltzer

The Simsbury Seminars
edited by Rosa Castella, Lluis Farré, and
Carlos Tabbia

MELTZER IN SÃO PAULO

Edited by

Marisa Pelella Mélega

with Alfredo Colucci, Célia Fix Korbivcher,
Alicia Beatriz Dorado de Lisondo, Martha Maria de
Moraes Ribeiro, and Paulo Cesar Sandler

Published for
The Harris Meltzer Trust
by
KARNAC

Published for The Harris Meltzer Trust by
Karnac Books Ltd, 118 Finchley Road, London NW3 5HT

Series editor Meg Harris Williams

British Library Cataloguing in Publication Data
A C.I.P. for this book is available from the British Library

 ISBN 978 1 78220 4657

Edited, designed and produced by The Bourne Studios
www.bournestudios.co.uk
Printed in Great Britain

www.harris-meltzer-trust.org.uk
www.karnacbooks.com

CONTENTS

Alfredo Colucci graduated as a medical doctor and psychiatrist from Ribeirão Preto Medical School, University of São Paulo. He was director of the Department of Medical Psychology and Psychiatry, FAMEMA State Medical College from 1966 to 1975, and clinical director of the Psychiatric Hospital of Marília, São Paulo, from 1966 to 1977. He is a member and (since 1989) a training analyst of the Brazilian Psychoanalytic Society of São Paulo.

Célia Fix Korbivcher is a child analyst and a training and supervising analyst of the Brazilian Psychoanalytic Society of São Paulo (SBPSP). Her attention is focused on the study of autistic phenomena in neurotic patients. She has published papers in local and international journals, including the *IJP*, and is author of *Autistic Transformations: Bion's Theory and Autistic Phenomena* (Karnac, 2013). In 2004 she was awarded the Parthenope Bion Thalamo International Prize and in 2005 the Frances Tustin Memorial Prize.

Alicia Beatriz Dorado de Lisondo is a training analyst of the Brazilian Psychoanalytic Society of São Paulo (SBPSP) and the

Study Group of Psychoanalysis of Campinas (GEP Campinas). She is co-coordinator of the adoption and parental group of the SBPSP and a full member of their research group on autism, and representative for children and adolescents for GEP Campinas with FEPAL (Latin American Psychoanalytic Federation), where she received a prize for her paper 'Reverie review'. 'Applications of the knowledge of psychoanalysis to the work in an institutional psychopathological service' received the Bleger Prize of the Psychoanalytic Association of Argentina (APA) in 1976.

Marisa Pelella Mélega is a psychiatrist, psychoanalyst in private practice, and a training analyst and supervisor at the Brazilian Psychoanalytic Society of São Paulo. She founded the Mother-Infant Relationship Study Centre in 1987, in São Paulo, receiving accreditation from the Centro Studi Martha Harris, in Rome. She is the author of *Pos Autismo: Uma Narrativa Psicanalitica* (Imago, 1999), *Post-Autism: A Psychoanalytical Narrative with Supervisions by Donald Meltzer* (Harris Meltzer Trust, 2014), *Imagens Oníricas e Formas Poéticas: Um Estudo da Criatividade* (Pasavento, 2015), *O Olhar e a Escuta para Compreender a Primeira Infância* (Casa do Psicólogo, 2008), *Looking and Listening* (Harris Meltzer Trust, 2012), and 'An amplified psychoanalysis', in: *Teaching Meltzer: Modes and Approaches*, edited by Meg Harris Williams (Harris Meltzer Trust, 2015). E-mail: pmelega@ uol.com.br

Martha Maria de Moraes Ribeiro is a supervising and training analyst at the Brazilian Psychoanalytic Society of Ribeirão Preto (SBPRP) and a full member of the Brazilian Psychoanalytic Society of São Paulo (SBPSP). She graduated in medicine at the University of São Paulo in 1970 and worked as an endocrinologist until 1984. In 1984 she was one of the founders of the Psychoanalytic Study Group of Ribeirão Preto and was Director of its Institute of Psychoanalysis when it became a full society in 2005. She has served on the editorial boards of major psychoanalytic journals in Brazil, such as *Revista Brasileira de Psicanálise* and *Berggasse, 19*. She teaches, practises, and supervises in Ribeirão Preto.

Paulo Cesar Sandler is a training analyst for the Brazilian Psychoanalytic Society of São Paulo (SBPSP). He is a psychiatrist at the institute of physical rehabilitation at the faculty of Medicine, University of São Paulo (FMUSP), and an honorary associate of the Accademia Lancisiana, Rome. He is author of *The Language of Bion: A Dictionary of Concepts* (Karnac, 2010), *A Clinical Application of Bion's Concepts* (Karnac, 2009–2013), *An Introduction to Bion's* A Memoir of the Future (Karnac, 2014–2015), and translator of works by Bion, Meltzer, and Winnicott into Portuguese. E-mail: dr.pcsandler@gmail.com

In 1979 Meltzer was at São Paulo Psychoanalytic Society (SBPSP) with his wife Martha Harris, when they presented their work method of the 'psychoanalytic atelier'. Their view was that analytical training should begins with the observation of the mother–baby relationship, since observing and describing is the way to reach the meaning of the phenomena experienced in the consulting room.

Meltzer sees in the analytical process a natural history whose evolution takes place as a result of modifications in the transference following a sequence comparable to the development of the earliest object relations: from a dependency not tolerated and projected out, to an introjective dependence acknowledging the importance of the object and its freedom. The basis for this understanding comes from Klein, with the theory of the positions, splitting, projective identification, and the concreteness of psychic reality. For Meltzer, the analyst's main task is the creation of a setting in which the infantile transference processes of a patient can take on the shape of a quest for truth.

When he came back to São Paulo in 1989, Meltzer remarked on how much Bion's ideas had added to his clinical practice, and we can see this in his comments on each clinical case presented in this book.

Always starting from the observation and description of phenomena during the analytic session, he now emphasised the role of confusion rather than of instinctive conflicts as responsible for the disruption of emotional development. According to Meltzer, interpreting confusion is more functional than interpreting splitting processes as the conflict between the good and evil parts of a personality. Bion led us away from the ancient belief that man is a desperately bad animal, and that psychoanalysis refers to a conflict between good and evil in a personality. Meltzer regards Bion's direction as humanist, since he acknowledges that man is intelligent enough to see the problem, but not to solve it: consequently, he suffers from his confusion.

Meltzer started to view the analytical process not only as the description of phantasy life and defence mechanisms, but also in terms of the possibility of describing mental processes in the light of Bion's contributions. From this point on, the psychoanalyst's task became more interesting, and more complicated, according to Meltzer. It is interesting when the patient is engaged in the getting to know the way his mind works, but it is frustrating if the patient simply wants to be rid of his symptoms and his pain.

With regards to pain, helping the patient to get interested in its meaning increases his tolerance to it, according to Meltzer. He also states that joining the patient in pain is not very useful.

As for the thought disorders he tracks during his supervisions, Meltzer emphasises the need for a careful study of the patient's language and the imagery of his dreams. In this way it is possible to uncover a huge area of self-delusion which has nothing to do with lies, as well as a confabulation area which also has nothing to do with lies, and an area full of transformations in hallucinosis, which has nothing to do with the hallucinatory processes of psychotic disturbances.

During these seminars, we watched Meltzer's interventions indicating a deep understanding of the patient's psychic structure. For me, such interventions are the result of a complete assimilation of Klein's work, as well as of some expansion by post-Kleinians, mainly Bion and Meltzer. Concepts which have been found especially useful are: Meltzer's expanded view of identification, which distinguishes projective identification, intrusive identification, and adhesive identification – the latter described together with Esther Bick. Another important concept in Meltzer's mind model is the combined object, which in its primitive form consists in breast and nipple, coalescing with the idea of mother and father in a sexual intercourse. It was a concept discovered by Klein in her work with Richard and according to Meltzer, this discovery had an aesthetic impact on Klein, due to its novelty. The concept of the combined object is necessary for the comprehension of the origin of creativity in the individual, for his capacity for symbol-formation. Another dynamic aspect of the object is Meltzer's proposal of the 'toilet-breast'.

This book presents a number of the cases that Meltzer discussed during several clinical seminars in São Paulo on his visits in 1989 and 1996, and one from his visit to Uruguay in 1993; some cases were also followed in group supervisions in Oxford.

The first is that of a 39-year-old woman with a manic-depressive personality. Her case was presented to Meltzer by Marisa Pelella Mélega at a seminar on dreams in Sao Paulo in 1989. Meltzer always emphasises the need to learn to read the total (visual and verbal) symbolism in dreams. A series of dreams are presented from the first half-year of analysis and are interpreted together by Meltzer as a 'dream narrative', showing how they interlink into a single symbolic thread.

The second chapter, by Celia Fix Korbivcher, describes a 25-year-old woman with an issue of voyeurism. In this seminar, Meltzer 'fishes up' the infantile transference in the patient's oscillation between claustrophobic depression and excited nymphomania associated with projective identification into the mother's vagina. This is suggested through the patient's voyeurism, a phantasy of intrusion into the internal mother as elaborated in Meltzer's book *The Claustrum*. Meltzer recommends following the theme of voyeurism in this patient, who is however not considered by him to be in a seriously fixed state of illness.

The next chapter, 'Emergence from living in projective identification', by Martha Maria de Moraes Ribeiro, concerns a patient whom Meltzer believes to have been on the borderline between schizophrenia (the world of delusion which is inaccessible to psychoanalysis) and projective identification. After eight years the analyst has succeeded in making contact with non-schizophrenic parts that have been living in projective identification, with a chance of drawing the patient back into the world of emotional reality where analysis is possible.

In 'A countertransference experience with an eleven-year-old-boy', by Alicia Beatriz Dorado de Lisondo, we meet an child who thinks he is an adult, owing to his confusion between social hierarchic concepts of acceptability and a concept of psychic development. In his relation with the analyst we see him testing the structural solidity of the analyst's interest in him, rather than just her caring for him, as she observes through an interesting countertransference insight.

In 'Premonitions of the depressive position' by Alfredo Colucci, the patient is waiting for the birth of his wife's baby, misidentifying this birth with the end of his analysis, yet with a certain realistic psychological premonition as Meltzer points out when he remarks that the material demonstrates very nicely the moment that is crucial in any analysis: the threshold of the depressive position.

In the next seminar, 'Overcoming a preformed transference', presented by Paulo Cesar Sandler, Meltzer listens to the material for a long time, and eventually expresses the view that behind the linguistic facility of the patient lies a significant disorder in thinking, typical in people whose incapacity to think is hidden beneath a facility for smooth talking. It is a camouflage technique based on a language of fashion and clichés. Rather than being wrapped in a 'false self' however this patient appears more like a child. The concept of the preformed transference is explained.

'Thought disorder from living in a claustrophobic world', by Marisa Mélega, describes a young woman who complains of a longstanding panic syndrome. Meltzer begins by stating that 'Panic is the past presented undigested, not thinking.' The patient lived in a claustrophobic world, entertaining herself with concrete thoughts of disasters that had no basis in reality. According to Meltzer such patients who suffer from thought disorders rather than developmental disorders are always very argumentative and tiresome to work with.

Finally in 'Confusional states and a childish erotic transference', Marisa Mélega presents a case which was followed by Meltzer over several years. The patient has an intense childlike erotic transference to the analyst as a maternal figure, resulting in zonal and geographical confusions. Meltzer differentiates this childish eroticism from sadomasochism, and differentiates the concept of pre-oedipal from pregenital states of mind. As the depressive position is approached we see the difference between *being* confused and *feeling* confused. Different types of dream symbols are discussed. Although the patient is a prolific dreamer she has problems moving from an acting mode to a thinking mode of creative, autonomous symbol-formation.

We apprehended from these supervisions that the analyst's job is of a primarily descriptive nature, rather than an explanatory nature, as the function of interpretation used to be considered. We do not explain anything; we simply give our opinions. As for dreams, Meltzer emphasises that the manifest content is not at all manifest: we cannot find out the meaning of any dream until we discover the symbol-formation within it. This is comprised not only by its pictorial aspect but also by the language content which accompanies the dream and its description in the session.

The authors of this book are unanimous in acknowledging Meltzer as a spontaneous thinker whose thinking embodies learning from experience. His generosity, his humour, and his life wisdom impressed all the people who worked with him in a highly positive way.

Marisa Pelella Mélega

CHAPTER ONE

Narrative of a dream life
(1989)

Marisa Pelella Mélega

B efore describing the case of Louise, which was presented at two clinical seminars with Meltzer in Brazil in 1989, and later in supervision in London (1990), I would like to say a few words about my interest in dreaming. This started a long time ago with my personal analysis, when I realised how much I used to dream – possibly because I had someone to talk to, my analyst – and I wrote down over one hundred dreams. At that time (the 1970s and 80s) the Psychoanalytic Society of São Paulo tended not to pay much attention to dreams dreamt during the analysis process. However I was also working with patients who brought me dreams, which motivated me to study and try to understand them. In our daily life we often omit trying to understand the dreams which appear so strangely; they seem absurd, chaotic, the manifestation of fears or repressed desires, and so on. A dream is inaccessible to reading with the same 'alphabet', the same signs and language we employ whilst we are awake.

The issuing of Meltzer's *Dream Life* (1983) was of great profit for the analyst interested in the phenomenon of dreaming. In this book, Meltzer traces the psychoanalytic view of dreams from Freud onwards, and then he develops a new dream theory especially based on Bion's 'A theory of thinking' (1962), where Bion claims that the meaning of emotions is the very core of the symbolic mind: from sensorial and emotional data 'alpha function' – a function of personality – would generate mental contents he called 'alpha elements'. These are predominantly visual images, dream-thoughts. Since then dreaming has acquired a new status in psychoanalytic practice, as unconscious thinking. This type of thinking is based on emotional experiences; it is a preverbal thinking process, resembling a child's play or a baby's movements. Night dreams result from our unconscious thinking, which is in fact a process going on day and night, and have some specific characteristics; the 'day leftovers' (Freud) are frequently a clue for the interpretation of an emotional experience.

In *Dream Life* Meltzer explores the relationship between visual symbolic forms and verbal forms; he explains two levels on which symbols are formed. One acts from the depths of the unconscious that transmits emotional states through projective identification. The other acts from the conscious level, superimposing words on the underlying music in order to communicate information about the external world. The interpretation of a dream during analysis is an example of the transformation of dream images into verbal language to formulate the meaning. For Meltzer, symbols are generated by internal objects rather than by the self, as was thought before Klein and Segal.[1] He sees both the psychoanalytic process and the narrative of a patient's dream as having a natural history, similar to the natural history of an individual. This becomes manifest in the infantile transference, which the analyst is expected to be able to receive in the maternal transference. And in order to apprehend a dream, it is necessary to know its symbolic structure.

Meltzer tells a disappointing story regarding the practice of dream analysis that Freud inaugurated as being 'the royal road to the unconscious'. He believes that neglect of dream analysis is partly due to the absence of a technique for its exploration,

1   As described in his paper 'Beyond conscience', *Revista Brasileira de Psicanálise*, 26 (3), 1992.

as well as to analysts' resistance to deepening their emotional involvement in the transference–countertransference process.

When I heard Meltzer commenting on the material of Louise, I was surprised and impressed by his capacity to understand the symbolic structure of the dreams I presented to him, as well as their symbolic continuity. I learned that for Meltzer the work with dreams was central to his practice, and he was always very much at ease in understanding them. Perhaps this involves a real talent. We can now appreciate it at work in this seminar, which even today stirs a strong impression in me as it so deeply influenced my analytic practice.

Louise: first clinical seminar in Brazil

Louise had been in analysis with me for a year at the time of this seminar, which focussed on the interpretation of dreams. She was aged 39 and had a manic-depressive personality with homosexual tendencies. Such tendencies can lead to instability in sexual identification, and to confusion between male and female. Eight dreams that occurred over a period of five months were discussed with Dr Meltzer.

When I met Louise at our first consultation, she looked old, thin, lifeless, feminine and fragile in her red dress; there was a slight smell of mould. She told me about a gastric ulcer and the tests she was having. We arranged to start analysis after the summer holidays.

The first session was marked by her telling me about various setbacks she had had. It was difficult for her to believe in either good or bad luck. She could only believe in an implicit hypothesis of fate. (A few months later, she told me about a setback she and the man she later married had suffered; at the time, she promised she would marry him should that difficulty be resolved.) Then she began to relate her life story. Her parents had been immigrants, and arrived in Brazil when her mother was six months pregnant with Louise. She described herself as 'a very good child', very obedient. She did not give her mother much trouble and would not ask for much (perhaps she could not play the role of a child?). When she was nine, her sister, who has their mother's name, was born. A few months later in the analysis, she told me her mother had had three miscarriages before her sister was born.

She helped her mother to babysit her sister. Some family friends considered her very strong, but they also warned her parents about her possible feelings of jealousy (which her parents had not noticed so far). A memory comes to mind from this time, when Louise was playing at shops, selling fruit. Her grandfather (her father's father) wanted to take a banana, but he would have to pay for it, according to the rules of the game. Her father intervened and smacked her. From that moment she became so disturbed and difficult that her mother's milk even dried up. She and her father could not get along well any more. Before this episode, they had been very close friends, and she adored leaving home early with him every day to open his bakery.

The following session she wanted to tell me not just the bad things of her life, but also the good ones. She talked about going to parties and attending artistic activities. She talked about her husband (they had no children). She also mentioned 'empty people smelling of mould', and 'crazy love affairs'. She even said that she considered herself to be homosexual, for she had had several affairs with her colleagues (later she told me of an affair with a pregnant married woman, and of another one who had got married and now she and her husband share an office with Louise). All this happened before she legally separated from her husband.

When talking to me, she is cautious and expresses herself somewhat slowly. A certain resistance to a psychological relationship prevails; she would rather talk about her physical indispositions – fatigue, headaches, stiff neck, menstrual cramps, stomachache and drowsiness – all of them interfering with her social and professional performance. It seems to me that these anxieties are experienced on the somatic, non-symbolical level. She can communicate verbally very well, when she is not assaulted by such anxieties, and demonstrates a certain sophistication in her taste and choice (clothes, household affairs, food). She is also very sensitive to beauty and the arts. She would like to have a small antique shop.

The rhythm of attendances and absences in the analytical situation is an established one. Her sessions are from Monday to Thursday, and on the first session of the week she usually complains of severe headaches. She claims that she has had these headaches for years, and they usually happen on Fridays and are followed by dreams. The interpretation of the primary scene and of catastrophic experiences felt on the physical level when separations are approaching does not seem to make sense to her.

After one month of analysis, she starts telling me her dreams.

A narrative of eight dreams

Dream 1 (on a Monday session): *My sister returned from Germany, and my father bought her a car. I cried out loudly 'That's unfair, unfair!'* She woke up frightened.

Dream 2: *I am on a couch, which is placed across the room, and you are by my side. Your hands are on my knees and you are trying to seduce me, saying you need affection and attention. And in a sexual manner. In the second part of the dream, it is you but you have dark skin, narrow shoulders, and seem a feeble, decrepit person …* (she pauses to think) *no, a small, fragile person, and the place was a different one, with other people and we were sitting and talking.*

At the next session, she recounts a dream involving an umbrella and a fowl. She says she hated this dream.

Dream 3: *It was a huge fowl, with a bare neck. Was it a guinea fowl? Or something else? I took it to a house on Augusta Street to be cooked, but it was not a food shop; it looked like an umbrella-shop near the house where I spent my childhood* (which in fact was miles away).

She associates the dream with her dislike of eating poultry. She had not eaten meat as a child, and only started eating it recently. When she was small, her mother would ask her to go to the butcher's to buy some meat, but she could not stand the smell, which made her breathless. She associates that with a childhood incident. A friend of hers approached her holding a chicken by the neck, and she was so startled that she ran away, bumped her head against a post, and fainted. She also remembered that when she was at secondary school, she was asked to observe an animal. She chose to observe chickens, and for a year she took care of three chicks. Two of them became beautiful hens, and one died. She found it weird to have chosen to observe an animal she disliked.

Donald Meltzer: Was it a living fowl?

Marisa Melega: I don't know. Maybe.

DM: Three dreams in two sessions?

MM: Yes.

DM: One is related to her relationship with her father, the second is about having sexual intercourse with her mother; the third one is related to the breast, that she has decided to become vegetarian. This is the beginning of the analysis. Who has referred the patient to you?

MM: A colleague.

DM: A male or a female one?

Meltzer explains that he wants to know it because it is important in this case. The dreams that appear at the beginning of the analysis express dissatisfaction at being with the analyst. There is a possibility that the patient had wanted to have analysis with someone else, and this person has referred her to another (her father has ejaculated on her mother in order to get rid of her). Mother was pleased to have a baby to suck her breast because she was in need of attention, but for the baby it was not an agreeable experience. This is not a very good beginning for an analysis. In a certain way it is amazing – umbrella, parasol – it gives the impression that the breast has another form that has a protective function, but it is not this that she is seeking. It is quite a packed beginning.

MM: I'm going to skip part of the material as it is incomplete.

DM: All material is incomplete.

MM: There is a week when she doesn't come, because she is dehydrated. On the following week, in spite of being sick, she comes, but I don't have any material. Here is the next dream:

Dream 4: *She is walking on a dirt track with water on either side. The road ends up at a lake, which has clear and shallow water, full of walking-sticks. They were dropped in the lake by elderly people strolling by who had difficulty in passing. Someone seemed to have the idea of rescuing the walking-sticks.*

DM: This seems to be a reference to vomit. She's vomiting all her father's sticks. She thinks that this breast is unpleasant to suck because the nipple is very phallic for her. Coming back to the person who was taking the chicken by the neck, scaring her, making her hit her head on the post. There is another side of this: that is to say, the three chicks that she raised. These were the babies. What seems to be appearing in the analysis is the confusion on the part of the object, who needs attention, who is scared. The material reflects a lot of mess. She vomits her discomfort. It seems that she's close to a woman and this is, at the same time, both exciting and quite confusing. What disturbs her mostly is the chicken neck–penis. She has become vegetarian in order to avoid this penis. It is very confusing and primitive material, indeed.   '

MM: In the dream, there was someone who was helping her to retrieve these walking-sticks in order to restore them. She comments that she always wanted to have an antique shop.

DM: An antique shop is a trinket store where people throw away what they don't want any more.

MM: During part of July, I replaced some sessions because of the patient's trip abroad. For the patient it was a revelation that the analyst was available to replace them. She was very grateful.

DM: I'm surprised that she has become so grateful to you rather than seeing you as needing the replacement sessions. Because in her dream the analyst is the one who needs affection.

MM: At the first session after her holidays, she was euphoric, coming quite willingly to meet an idealised analyst. She had sent me a postcard, however I hadn't received it yet. She asked about the possibility of other replacement sessions owing to her trip. I told her I would look into the possibilities. After this, the patient kept quiet and started to become sleepy. I told her that with the non-replacement of the sessions there seems to be an analyst who frustrates, and that for her an illusion (of an idealised analyst) is broken.

DM: This session is another attempt at false reparation regarding the analyst. This effort has left her worn out. This links to my doubt concerning her gratitude for the analyst.

MM: It follows a difficult month, a lot of headache, stomach-ache, drowsiness. She seems very disappointed.

DM: She is behaving like a mother who is feeling guilty for having left her baby, and when she comes back, she fondles the baby, who doesn't care. Then comes the blame. The baby treats the breast as if it were his own breast, and not as if it belonged to the mother.

In the second dream, when the analyst is trying to seduce her, the picture shows the patient seeing the analyst as if she were a baby. This is what we call reversal of perspective. She is seeing the analyst as blaming her and with the feeling that the analyst is not going to forgive her for having left on vacation.

MM: Another session, a Monday. The patient said she was depressed. She doesn't know how to do analysis, she considers giving up. With another analyst, she spent a year sleeping. I interpret how scared she is about the things she is feeling about herself in the analysis. She remembers another dream:

Dream 5: *I was in a room lying down as if I were ill, and my mother was nearby; I was my actual age, and my mother and father, who arrived right after work, were younger. My father kisses my mother and pinches her, embraces her and becomes sexually excited. He leaves to take a shower and prepares to lie down for intercourse. He calls my mother, but she seems to want to stay with me, and my father gets angry at her delay. Thus, his erection disappears.* (She uses a vulgar word for 'erection'.)

DM: In this dream, her parents are younger than her. This is a reversed perspective. If you follow the reversal: there are two children – a girl and a boy – and when their mother comes back, they make clear to her the kind of sexual game they were playing in her absence. The game is that the boy acts as a tyrant in relation to the girl. However, in the mother's presence, he can't act as a tyrant. In the transference, she is depressed because she observes that in her absence, the analyst could have used her session hours to play sexual games with her husband. A reversed Oedipus complex.

MM: The patient has lost her idealisation.

DM: It has a sense of giving up being a mother. Now she notices that her children will never forgive her for having left.

So, she is giving up being a mother. This is what happens with mothers who abandon their children. We have an indication in this material that this woman doesn't know how to forgive. The children will forgive their mother, but will go on playing these sexual games. Here she thinks that the analyst is not going to forgive her, pretending she hasn't received the postcard. She wants the analyst to replace the sessions, and the analyst doesn't make such an offer; she simply interprets to her.

MM: At the following session, I told her I had received her postcard.

DM: This is like a mother and a child when they are separated. When the mother comes back, the child doesn't 'recognise' her immediately. The mother hopes her child will listen to the good news she wants to tell her.

MM: She sent a postcard from a town where there were lots of Christmas decorations. She says that didn't visit the Nazi torture museum. She'd rather see more beautiful things.

DM: In general, this kind of museum (sadomasochist facts) appeals to children. She is trying to make peace with the analyst in this way.

MM: In the following session, we talked about her way of investigating a misunderstanding she had had with a colleague at her office. She says she is not to blame for the quarrels and arguments she was having.

DM: What was the misunderstanding about?

MM: Something related to management.

DM: It seems that she doesn't feel guilty for creating confusion. It was her father who created confusion. She and her mother were about to get along well when her father called her mother and created all this confusion. And we come back to the mother–baby situation. The baby was almost about to forgive the mother. Men are the ones who create confusion, always calling women.

MM: She says that madness was never discussed in her family. She had a schizophrenic uncle, who at the end of his life was hospitalised on her recommendation.

DM: She had thrown her uncle out of the family, and then she felt guilty. She asks about her brother. Everything that happens makes her feel guilty, but afterwards she has a way to deal with it: men are the guilty ones.

MM: In another session, she tells me about a lorry that hit her car. She feels it was quite unfair. When the driver admitted his guilt, things got better. Her father always blamed her when she banged her car.

DM: She is generous and ready to forgive, but she wants the driver to admit the guilt, which is his. She got free of her husband and her uncle too.

MM: In another session, the patient ran into an eleven-year-old girl, but it was not her fault. She was on her way to take care of her parents' cat, very unwillingly, while they were away. While driving there, she ran into the girl. What made her feel guilty was the fact that she was mad at being obliged to take care of the cat.

DM: She was obliged to take care of the cat. She is trying to invent the facts. The main thing is that she doesn't know why she should feel guilty.

MM: In the first month of analysis, she constantly mentioned that she was the victim of different things. For example, she had been the victim of several thefts.

DM: This is the state of mind of the depressed psychotic. It is the situation of those who go from a doctor to doctor, not believing in the diagnosis. At the same time, they are very dependent and disintegrate during their analytical vacations. It is hard establishing the analytic situation, establishing contact with them.

MM: I would like to ask: How do dreams inform us about the patient's mental structure? What does she do with the emotional experience? What transformations is she making?

DM: This kind of patient acts in the transference. This is what she is doing when she brings dreams, like the postcard. She supposes this will please the analyst. It is very difficult involving her in an emotional relationship. It is immediately transformed into action. The dreams reveal the trick mechanisms, manic defence, hypocrisy, and false reparation. Indeed, the emotionality is very small. She is adept at inventing arguments, at destroying the truth. She relates to the analyst in a hypocritical way. Her transference is dominated by confusion from a reversal of the dependence relationship – the analyst is a child and she is the mother.

In the background is a strong homosexual tendency and a powerful personality. Although in my opinion, no homosexual material has appeared as yet. The transference doesn't seem full of eroticism.

MM: And what about the physical symptoms?

DM: They give the impression that she comes with diffuse hypochondria that quickly started to show up. Diffuse hypochondria was immediately projected on the transference. The analyst was turned into her mother. In her dream, the analyst is well, but then becomes debilitated. A reversal of the transference situation. The analyst became smaller, as well as her parents. What impresses is her insistence on being 'right' and the hypocrisy with which she expresses it. One never knows when this kind of patient is going to disappear from the therapy.

MM: I have three further dreams to relate:

Dream 6: *I was in an old house with my parents. My father is welcoming a painter, who looks like a tramp, and invites him to stay for the night. I know he doesn't really mean it. So after my shock at seeing my father inviting a beggar into the house, I take the initiative and I tell the beggar not to stay.*

Dream 7: *A handsome policeman (an actor I always liked) came into my house on a motorbike.*

Dream 8: *I was with a friend near a swimming-pool, and my friend installed a protective cover over the pool, so that the leaves brought by the wind wouldn't fall into it (to keep the pool clean). The next scene is you and I, and I was putting rice into a small pan. As it cooked, it was going to spill over. You and the others looked at me critically.*

DM: This dream concerning the swimming pool seems to be linked to the sticks, the vomit. In the other part, she's going to be criticised. Everything is related to the fact of having lost the session. It's also related to separating the dirt, but she is leaving the dirt to Marisa, in a typical manic-depressive way. She thinks she is fine, but she is criticised. False reparation.

The tramp dream shows she is convinced she knows what is going on in her father's mind. She tries to maintain her belief system that she is right. Her needy beggar-painter part is being received in the analysis, but she insists on keeping up the idea of cruel parents and analyst. She comes late to the session, but confesses she had arrived early and stayed in the car manicuring her nails. She can't admit that she wants to be received. She can't admit the needy-beggar part.

There are different kinds of omniscience. It is difficult to distinguish them by their manifestations alone. They may be based on projective identification; or on identification with the internal object – the delusion of clarity of insight – and then there is transformation in hallucinosis. My hunch is that here it is mainly a state of projective identification with the mother. She feels she is the family mother who knows what is happening in the father's mind. It is difficult to distinguish.

Second seminar about the dream narrative

During the second clinical seminar, with a larger group of participants, Dr Meltzer asked for the dreams to be read out, together with the patient's associations, in order to discuss them and to organise the dream material in terms of an ongoing narrative. The eight dreams are read out, and in the course of the discussion I supply the patient's associations.

Donald Meltzer: This dream narrative starts with her complaining about how unfair it was that her sister should have got a car, and ends with her about to be criticised because she has spilled the rice. And in the middle of the story, there is much evidence of reversal of dependence: the analyst wants affection and sex, the parents are younger than she is and interfere in her sexuality, and so on.

It is important to know that this patient used to be a vegetarian, and it is also important that during the course of this therapy, in May, there was an episode of vomiting with dehydration, and she missed a session. I must also mention that during the analytic term she went on holiday, and sent Marisa a postcard that had not arrived when she returned for her first session. Marisa clarifies that the patient went on holiday three weeks before the analyst's holiday.

So we have the dream in which she is younger than her parents, and she interferes with their sexuality because mummy wants to stay with her, and the session before Marisa received her postcard. It is also important to mention that we know little about her history. But in her previous therapy, which lasted one year, she had spent the whole year sleeping on the couch. And we may presume that she slept in her parents' room for quite a long time.

Participant: Why does Dr Meltzer presume the patient was sleeping in her parents' room for such a long time?

DM: I think this material of reversal and of sleeping for a year in analysis suggests a child in her parents' bedroom, living in the midst of sexuality, over and over. She can hear her mother say: 'No, the child is still awake.' The child in the parents' room had two choices: either she interferes in the parents' intercourse by making it clear she is awake, or she participates in her parents' intercourse in a masturbatory way, pretending she is asleep.

For the first two dreams, there are no particular associations. The dream about the enormous fowl however has important associations. [The analyst relates the associations, given above.] You have this image of an enormous fowl taken by its bare neck, hanging down; the impression of a woman with her hand on the penis hits her like a blow in the head, and she runs into this post like a penis and knocks herself out. But it isn't the sight of the penis that is a shock to her. It is the sight of the penis being held in the girl or woman's hand. It's important that this penis is attached to an enormous fowl: you can see how the penis and scrotum are confused with the nipple and breast. Now, in the dream, this enormous fowl is being taken to be cooked, but in fact it was to a shop that sold umbrellas. And that leads on to the next dream where the umbrella comes back as a walking-stick. In between these two dreams was an episode in which she vomited to the point of dehydration and missed the session. So you can see how the dream about the old people's walking-sticks in the water is connected with vomiting in the toilet. And what she was vomiting up was all these umbrella-penises, these necks of the fowl that had turned into umbrellas that she swallowed up and then vomited.

In the dream she thought of somebody rescuing these walking-sticks to restore them to the old people – an idea of reparation – but in her association she connects that with the idea she always had of keeping a little antique shop. Now that is a little incident that looks like a reparative impulse, but you can see, in fact, it's a scavenging impulse: to get back all these walking-sticks that had been thrown away, and then she would sell them in her little antique shop. So, it's not really a reparative move: it's a manic move, what Melanie Klein called 'mock reparation'.

Now after that dream, we come to a point in which the analyst's holidays are approaching, and she decides she's going on a holiday with a sister, presumably the same sister who in the dream was given the car and the patient said it was unfair.

We are confronted by the patient with this decision as is a sort of *fait accompli* because the sister had already sent her the air ticket and so on. Because this will be a three-week break before the analyst's break and so will make for a tremendously long break, the analyst offers her extra sessions to make up for some she would miss, and the patient seemed to be very touched and grateful. Then after the double break as it were, telling her about the interesting places she'd been to and asking it she'd received the postcard which she had not yet done, she asked about further replacement sessions which the analyst said she would have to think about, she couldn't say immediately. The patient then became very sleepy and said she felt empty, and settled into depression.

That is a very interesting episode because in keeping with this patient's reversal of the dependence, she behaves exactly like her parents, who went off on a holiday, leaving the children alone or in the care of somebody else, and expecting the children to be delighted when they come back. They expect the children to want to hear all about the lovely time they had, so pleased with the postcards they received from them, and so on. The patient behaves just like parents who know absolutely nothing about how children feel about separation. And what happens as a consequence of the analyst's not having received the postcards, and not immediately agreeing to replace some of the missed sessions, is that she collapses into a depressed state, exactly like the mother who doesn't understand anything about children and feels absolutely crushed and rebuffed when the children, instead of being delighted, turn their backs on her and are unhappy and resentful, and so on. She became very difficult after this period when the analyst's holiday disappointed her, a good mummy whose children don't appreciate her ...

And it was in that context that she had this dream in which her parents were younger, her father was flirting with her mother and wanting to have intercourse, but mother didn't want to leave her child. So father lost his erection. And it was in the context of telling that dream (with its idea that 'They are behaving like a couple of adolescents, really'), and being on bad terms with the analysis, that she was thinking of giving up the analysis and mentioned how she had slept through the year of analysis with the previous therapist.

There was a sort of threat of leaving, and then the analyst did receive the postcard, and the patient was very pleased, and revealed that the place she had gone to was a very nice highly decorated church, and next to it a museum of Nazi torture, a concentration camp museum. Now, following that session about the postcard and Nazi torture, the patient becomes very confused and preoccupied with proving that she was not guilty of everything that other people were guilty of. So, perhaps you will read this session because it is very important for insight into what underlies the manic-depressive state.

At this point let us remind ourselves of the sequence so far. It started with her being in a rage about her sister's being given a car by the father. And then we have all this material that indicates the inversion of dependence on the mother: that the mother is dependent on the baby; the mother wants sexual satisfaction and affection from the baby; the breast wants to be licked and sucked, and is seen as this enormous fowl with its big neck. And when the woman takes hold of this neck, it becomes a penis, and the patient is knocked down.

So we have some purely part-object material in which nipple and breast and penis and scrotum are completely confused. When it comes back to the question of feeding: penis and nipple make her vomit and fill the toilet with all these discarded penises, the walking-sticks in the lakes. And now the acting-out of going off on her holiday –sending the postcard, coming back like a stupid mother who expects the children to be delighted she is back. And the mention here of sleeping in the previous therapy, with the dream in which she interferes with the parents' sexual relationship, indicates having slept in the parents' bedroom. Now comes this interesting problem of guilt and who is guilty – it is the shock of seeing the parents banqueting on each other's bodies, and the unfairness of it, as in the first dream about the father giving the car to the sister. There is all this material about how it is unfair that I am hungry and mummy and daddy are feasting …

MM: In the previous session, we talked about her way of investigating and trying to prove that she is not guilty of the quarrels and confusions: that she participated in creating a misunderstanding, for instance, with her colleague. She says that insanity was not acknowledged in her family, and that her father's brother lived with them for many years: he was schizophrenic and debilitated, but nobody could mention this. If she ever mentioned her uncle's insanity, she provoked her father's hostility. Eventually on her doing he ended up in a hospital as a terminal case, and died. She felt guilty about this death.

DM: We can see here the nature of the argument: she knocks down a girl with the car, but she's not guilty. It's her parents who are guilty because they left her with the task of looking after the cat. And she didn't really want to look after the cat. And that put her in such a state of mind that she didn't drive carefully and knocked down the girl, so it was her parents' fault.

Translating that plot into family life, she did not want to have to look after little sister, so when her little sister got hurt, because she was busy playing and did not notice, it was her parents' fault for leaving her little sister to her care; translating the fact that she didn't want to sleep in her parents' bedroom. So, with her staying awake, interfering with her parents' intercourse, that's their fault. So, she pretended to be asleep so she could observe and participate in their intercourse, and that interferes with her sanity and development, and that's their fault.

Now we get the dream that shows precisely what happens in the parents' bedroom: the two different types of events – the one where she interferes, and the one where she participates. So, Marisa, read these two dreams over again, because they are so precise.

MM (reading the dream): *'I was in an old house with my parents. My father is welcoming a painter, who looks like a tramp, and invites him to stay for the night. I know he doesn't really mean it. So after my shock at seeing my father inviting a beggar into the house, I take the initiative and I tell the beggar not to stay.'*

DM: This is absolutely precise. First of all, you see the scene: father is about to get into bed with mother, and she sees his non-erect penis, but she knows what's going to happen as soon as he gets into bed – he's going to get an erection and is going to want to have intercourse with mummy. But then comes her omniscience, She knows what is going on, that he doesn't really want to get into bed with mummy. He doesn't really want have an erection, he doesn't really want to have intercourse with her; so she makes a fuss, and mummy takes her into bed and daddy sleeps elsewhere. That omniscient interference is exactly the omniscience with which she gets her uncle put into the mental hospital where he died. This state of mind of omniscience and the interference with her sexuality is blamed on the parents, because she didn't want to sleep in their bedroom, like she didn't want to look after the cat. Now, we get the next dream, which shows the other side of the picture, when she pretends to be asleep.

MM (reading the dream) : *'A handsome policeman (an actor I always liked) came into my house on a motorbike.'*

DM: The handsome policeman comes into her house on a motorbike, receiving into herself the erect handsome penis. Anything good that happened, she participated in, and anything bad that happened is not her fault, it's somebody else's. You see how the projective identification produces this reversal, this feeling of omniscience, knowing better than the parents, and this is the underlying story of manic-depressive states.

It is difficult to get a real analysis going with a manic-depressive patient.

It's from that level that the terrific zonal confusion occurs: a series of confusions – between penis, faeces, nipple, baby, and between mouth, anus, vagina. At part-object level, they are so interchangeable, and this is all in a fowl with its naked neck and the association of the girl holding the chicken. You can see where sometimes the combined part-object of nipple and breast, penis and scrotum, are absolutely indistinguishable, and I say this is pre-genital oedipal material because the parental intercourse is primarily the parents' feasting, eating one another, as evidenced here by a vegetarian inability to eat meat and so on. The story about the chicken and her hitting her head on the post strongly suggests that the most shocking sight was her mother sucking daddy's penis.

Then there's the dream about the walking-sticks and the lake which accompanied her vomiting experiences. A baby is sucking the breast where the nipple has become confused with the penis; let's steal the penis, not introject the breast (this is what I wrote in the paper on cyclothymic states).

MM: Can you say more about omniscience.

DM: Yes, we talked yesterday about how there are different kinds of omniscience that have a different basis. Now Dr Bion has described what is probably the most important type of omniscience. That is, omniscience based on transformation in hallucinosis, and in the book *Extended Metapsychology* [Meltzer, 1986], there is a case that illustrates how hallucination-transformations operate. The patient's perceptions of the outside world are taken in and immediately destroyed, expelled again, and the outside world becomes full of destroyed objects, perceived with absolute certainty. The other type of omniscience comes from projective identification, mainly with the patient looking out through mother's eyes and seeing the world with the wisdom of the internal mother, and I've written about this in a paper entitled 'The delusion of clarity of insight'. Another type of omniscience is really a type of stupidity due to the denial of psychic reality, a failure of imagination: what we call in English having a one-track mind.

Now, the psychological phenomenon that Dr Bion has described is very difficult to demonstrate to patients. There is confusion in the transference when the patient is convinced he knows what you are thinking and feeling towards him; it is extremely difficult to demonstrate to him that this is omniscient, because the evidence as he sees it is different from the evidence as you see it. You speak with one tone of voice, and he hears another tone of voice. You speak with one type of vocabulary, and it has a different meaning for him. It is difficult to take on the impasse. One of the reasons it is so difficult is that the patient goes quiet about it. His inner feeling is 'Oh, it's no use talking to you about that. You don't understand.' The same thing happens in marriages. There are certain areas that become silent, that cannot be discussed – where one or the other feels that the other person's state of mind is unapproachable. So, knowing that you get these silent areas, it's very difficult to say to the patient: 'There are things you do not talk to me about, because it feels too accusative.' This is simply added to the omniscient refusal to discuss the problem.

Participant: Why did the patient sleep all the time with the previous analyst?

DM: Drawing from this material, my image of her attempting to have analysis with a man analyst would be something like this: that she falls asleep, she has an erotic dream about him, and awakes with the feeling that he is not a suitable father for the child in herself, because he is always exposing her to the parental intercourse. She leaves him. I can imagine her even developing the conviction that he was schizophrenic like the uncle, and belonged in a mental hospital. I think it would be impossible for her to have analysis with a man. Had I seen this patient in consultation and known her history, I would certainly have sent her to a woman.

One of the troubles in this field is that with most patients you see in consultation you think analysis would be better with a woman. It is a very difficult field for men because it is much harder for them to listen and hold the maternal transference, and the constructive work in analysis generally takes place mainly in the maternal transference. Of course the male analyst's own analysis should have revealed to him and brought him to the same degree of integration with his femininity. But because in our culture, and also in the analytic world, the differentiation between a man's femininity and his homosexuality is so difficult to define, men have much more anxiety about their homosexuality than woman have about their masculinity or homosexuality. It is generally easier for a woman psychoanalyst to get in touch with her masculinity than it is for a man to get in touch with his femininity. A woman analyst who is not much in touch with her masculinity has difficulty being firm enough and strong enough in an analysis. But those qualities the analyst can delegate to her husband, to her supervisor, to somebody else outside the immediate, sequestered situation, and this will often suffice to strengthen the patient's feeling of being contained in the analysis. But a man who is not much in touch with his femininity cannot notice the maternal transference very well and experience it in the countertransference, and therefore tends to work in a more intellectual way that has less sensitivity for both him and for the patient. So it isn't at all surprising that psychoanalytic history has shown relentless development towards becoming a more feminine field. Certainly, very few men seem to be able to work happily with children. So, you women must be kind to us, poor men – we have a tough time with our patients.

Supervision in London

The following analytic sessions with Louise were presented at a group supervision in London in 1990.

First analytic session: Tuesday

Monday was a holiday in Brazil and Louise informed that she had spent the holiday in bed.

She speaks about her admission interview at one institute, and her cold. She had got wet in the rain, so she has an explanation for getting a physical illness without the need to consider her feelings. She doesn't know if she was hearing noises, music, but she seemed to drift in and out of sleeping and waking. Delirium while having a temperature?

But the dream was well defined: *I was in a place with narrow streets, like Venice, but streets without water. I had to find something, had to turn left, but there was no exit ... I didn't know whether it was the Mayor's office or the Embassy. I went in. There were steps, about eight, and a landing, more steps, another landing. Some very beautiful ruins appeared. I was surprised. People behind me were picking up some to take away. I didn't think it was right, and I was sorry they did it. There were statues of lions, of people, needing to be restored; a beautiful place.*

Her associations were that 'analysis is a restoration. I think I must have thought of the municipal offices because I did my income-tax return over the holidays. Turning left is something that drew my attention in the dream – people on the left, the political leftist party?

I tell her she's seeking something – the Monday session which we didn't have because of the holiday. (She had said on Thursday that she didn't like that holiday – spending such a long time without a session – she alludes to her tension over the interview, etc.). I thought of making up for the missed session, but I wouldn't have been able to, and she didn't ask for a session, but there was that allusion in the air. To the 'left' is the entrance to the analyst's room down the corridor. She has to turn left to reach the analyst's room from which, in the dream, there is no exit (there will be no toilet-breast contact) and she returns to the top, climbing the stairs and finding the ruins. She had no idea of their existence. For her, this had a repercussion of having interviews and not feeling well, of colds and tensions. I repeat that the streets are narrow, without water, a foreign city (seeking a session which is beyond her reach). She says that it wouldn't certainly be Venice, it would be more like Florence. There she had seen excavations, and she thought it's idiotic to excavate because you may find Roman ruins, as you are also interfering with what actually exists there. For example, look at the Piazza della Signoria.

I tell her that what she finds 'idiotic' is what is being excavated or examined by means of the interviews, and which results in making a mess of her analysis through illnesses and absences. I take up again her state of not knowing whether she was dreaming or awake and hearing noises (when she had a temperature?) as if in a state of drowsiness, which happens frequently in the sessions. She agrees, and I add that it was in one of those states of mind, regarding the 'distance' – of her analysis – since what was 'heard' without distinguishing what was happening here with me was like a girl hearing distantly what was taking place in the parents' room. She then remembers that the corridor leading to her house by way of the bakery was long and narrow, and there was a room, beside her parents', with a connecting door. This room belonged to her paternal grandfather for a long time, although she used to have that room. He was diabetic and frequently ill. He even had comas at night. He would fall off the bed, and her parents would help him. She used to hear those noises and voices. She says she frequently heard them because her grandfather and her father went to bed early (they had a bakery), while she and her mother remained awake until later.

I found myself imagining a highly stimulated girl who decided to be concretely isolated, and not only with drowsiness and sleep. Since she got divorced, some years ago, she has been living on her own. Again, in the session, I had the impression that when she's awake she can function, explaining and justifying her mental states by means of external circumstances, and in dreams she tells how she felt her experiences, and how they had snowballed into mental 'ruins'.

Second session: Wednesday

Louise arrives on time, lies down, and sighs: 'I'm very tired; yesterday I felt good until lunch time, then I had nausea and I vomited, I think it was a vegetable I ate – I'm not feeling well at all.' There is a long pause of fifteen minutes.

I say she probably vomited what she ate here yesterday, something strange and indigestible (I think of her dream in which there was no way out, when she went on her way climbing stairs and landings till she saw the ruins). I tell her that vomiting means walking the way back, expelling 'ruins' that she could not throw up during the session she missed because of the holiday (Monday), and such 'ruins' found their way out through the mouth.

She remains silent, still, and when I ask her what is going on, she does not answer. Twenty-five minutes went by. I recognise she has set up a barrier in order to isolate herself from the contact with me, possibly because she is scared of its consequences.

She says she cannot leave in such state.

I think she is acting by becoming still, not asking for help, not investigating what is going on inside her. It seems to me she already knows there is nothing to be done, she already knows I can do nothing. It would be a state of omniscience.

The session ends.

Third session: Thursday

She arrives on time. She lies down and tells me she felt bad the day before, having vomited all the afternoon. In a flash – maybe on the radio – she heard the phrase 'the right to know'. She felt it made sense and that it had something to do with her. When studying in the morning she fell asleep, and she thinks it was a sabotage of her own, in order not to learn. She then tells a dream: *A psychiatrist was walking along a road between a psychoanalyst and an entrepreneur.*

I say she possibly feels she is prohibited from learning, and I agree that her drowsiness is a curtain or a barrier forbidding any investigation at the moment. It seems to me this happened after the dream involving 'ruins', which led to several associations, such as imagining she was taking me along the corridor to get to know the rooms in her house: her grandfather's, her parents', etc. The feeling was of a child expecting to learn about her parents, until she closed the door saying 'that's enough now'.

She remained silent for a few minutes, and then she started talking about this grandfather, her father's father, whom she disliked, although he was the only grandparent she ever met; he was always criticising her mother whom he thought weak. Her mother used to tell her about her maternal grandfather, who was a nice fellow. The house had only two bedrooms, and her paternal grandfather occupied her bedroom, while she went to sleep with her parents. Then after some time (she cannot remember how long) she went to sleep in a different part of the house that was reached through a flight of steps. There were two bedrooms there: in one of them, her schizophrenic uncle slept; in the other one, the bakery's employees slept. They were all women, and she went to sleep with them. She recalls falling asleep on the couch, and her mother took her wrapped in a blanket to her bedroom. She was approximately eight years old at the time.

I thought it was interesting to notice the description of the house and the places where she used to sleep: first her parents' bedroom, then climbing the stairs to reach the employees' room. And also the dream involving 'ruins'.

Fourth session: Monday

She is five minutes late. She greets me, but does not look at me. She sighs. She tells me about her health, and that on Friday she had her third admission interview for the psychoanalytic institution. She had liked it and she had been more enthusiastic. Then she talks about a dream she had on Friday – or was it Saturday? She tries hard to remember when, and I ask her why she gives this so much importance. She says she wants to test her memory; she is worried about it. In the interview, she had said she was 40 and had pondered on this and then she had mentioned that she got an ulcer when she separated from her husband, and thought to herself: 'Imagine what I will get when I separate from my parents, when they die.'

It was on that night that she had the dream. I tell her that it is an attempt to place herself in time and also because it refers to our analytic work. She agrees.

The dream: *I was with my parents and a guide in a desert place, with Arabs* (like the women in Arabian dresses in the film *The Jewel of the Nile*). *We had to cross a mountain whose access was difficult, narrow. The guide places a rope attached to somewhere on the mountain and tests it, but it is not very firm. Then the solution appears of placing a piece of newspaper round the end, to give some kind of support – similar to the way a screw can be made to sit snugly in a hole in the wall. In this way, it was possible to climb and cross. Then I am in a very big place with various people and I hear something, I have a vision that my mother is hanging from the rope. I run, and a girl says: 'How red you are from running so much!'* (this sensation is strong in the dream), *and I say that it is because my mother is there. Then it's a different scene, not oriental any more; there are buildings; I see my mother hanging, and she is going to fall because she cannot hold on anymore. I think, is she going to fall in the street? On top of the cars? The idea is that it happened and she dies.* I wake up in distress.

After the dream, she says, she was only able to calm down when she went to see her mother and found her well, fit and active.

The transcription that I made resulted in a series of small clarifications she gave to some of my inquiries. The dream seems to tell me a little more of her story. She is going up a 'mountain' with her parents, and in the end she passes through the entry where there is a 'cut' (her words). When the scene changes I associate this with what she told me about her house, the room where she slept with her parents, and how she then went further up, to a higher place, with stairs. She agrees and thinks about the terrible feeling she had when she found she could not remember parts of *The Jewel of the Nile*.

I remind her that it has to do with how she described that part of her infancy where she said she couldn't remember how the change of room took place – remaining wiped out. And I remind her that she feels disturbed thinking that her memory is failing her; but actually, she is able to recognise that this is happening (she is also trying to see her responsibility in rela-tion to her clients). In this way she shows some movements of progress and can imagine separating from her parents and losing them for good, through death.

The image of the mother hanging from a cord seems to me something like a plucked bird fastened by the throat as in the other dream – now the mother–breast? Is she suffering because she recognises her and imagines her death? I associate this with the separation (weaning) from the breast at weaning which she told me was traumatic (she was taken to a neighbour and left there for two days without seeing her mother).

The overcoming of the difficult access suggests birth with the mother separated and hung up (on the umbilical cord?). Then the mother is the baby (and the inversion continues), in the light of the present experiences of progress and of acceptance by the institution. It is suggestive of all of this.

Donald Meltzer: Preoccupied with her memory. She is going to die, and wakes up in anguish, and then goes to see her mother. She is worried about both her parents. She feels bad when she realises she can't remember parts of her dream; and that if she loses her memory she can lose clients. This is the context of the dream. It is a dream of being taken to her mother's breast. Following the analytical process and the way she is developing, she has recovered from these first anxieties, claustrophobia, and hypochondria. And now she is outside her mother's body. And the problem is coming to the breast. And immediately the idea of weaning arises, the death of the breast, the death of her parents, and it becomes difficult to attach herself to a nipple because it is going to die one of these days.

In this dream, it is very important to understand the question of 'the newspaper'. It is placed around a point of the mountain, and this allows the fixation of the rope. This has an unrealistic aspect, if we think of mountains and ropes, but it has some sort of meaning in terms of the baby's capacity to suck the nipple. This baby can be attached to the nipple if it has certain qualities that can be represented by the newspaper. Now, what are the qualities of a newspaper that make it capable of this representation? This is the puzzle!

I would say that the quality of a newspaper that is being represented here – allowing the baby to become attached to the nipple – is that the newspaper says, 'Nothing will happen to you, bad things happen to other people!'

That is why we read the papers: to know about all the bad things happening to other people. And this is very important. Then, this nipple says, 'Nothing can happen to you – you're mummy's baby!' But the result is, of course, that something can happen to the mother. It is the mother who is in danger: the breast is in danger, not the baby.

Marisa Melega: I was also thinking that the repairing with the paper is something very unreal, very shabby. Trying to make another connection implies that the mother dies, the breast dies.

DM: Yes, because there is a reversal. This is the reason why reassurance never works. If you reassure a patient that nothing bad is going to happen to him, this immediately intensifies his anxiety that something bad will happen to you, the analyst. Reassurance only transfers the self's anxiety to the object, but it does nothing for the anxiety itself. We can see in this dream, when the mother connects the baby to herself through reassurance (the paper), she assures her nothing bad can happen, but increases in her the feeling that something bad is going to happen to the mother.

MM: Such as weaning?

DM: Yes. As if weaning meant the death of the breast, rather than that it is the baby that is being taken away from the breast, and beginning to eat other foods. For the baby, the breast is dying. Interesting dream!

MM: It is interesting that all this series of dreams happened at a time when she is preparing to enter an institution.

DM: Yes. Why interesting?

MM: Because it seems to me it reactivated the primary experiences, and it threatens going on with this new link.

DM: In this material there is also something of the implication that it is the people 'on the left' who, even if they don't cause the ruin, at least steal bits and pieces, and contribute to the ruin. The people on the left would be your patients – who, like herself, pay you a low fee or, in some way, exhaust you or exploit you. That's the feeling.

She's been ill, and whether she's been ill because of psychosomatic illness or whether she's just got an ordinary physical illness, she's having a hypochondriacal dream. It's a dream in which you are the ill mummy who's invaded by all these children who take your things and pilfer and steal and damage and leave you in ruin. When she's ill, she's hypochondriacally identified with this damaged, exhausted mummy. That is the general situation she is in, but she denies she's one of these pilfering, stealing, leftist children. She pays her taxes. She goes for her interviews.

Now the point about this excavation business is that it's her way of saying that, in truth, the curiosity is pilfering because although you may find out some kind of information, you do damage by getting inside and excavating around looking for answers. The implication is that her tremendous intrusive curiosity is being projected onto the other children, the other patients, and she is the good girl.

It seems very appropriate that it's all noises coming from the parents' bedroom, and the fantasy of getting inside and exploring the mother's interior. She correctly understands that it is a stupid thing to do because it damages the mother. But she knows that what you should do if you have questions in your mind is to ask; and if mummy says they're too private and she doesn't want to tell you, then you mind your own business.

Although everybody does it, this arrangement about the bill – charging her less and giving her a receipt for less than she pays you – is nonetheless an item of suspicion to her. These are the noises that have replaced, in her memory, the noises of the parents' intercourse. But the answer is probably that she lives in a kind of vicarious projective identification with other people, has fantasies about them, identifies with them and with you, and although she says she and her mother went to bed early, what she doesn't say but probably means is that they went to bed together until daddy came, and then she would be put elsewhere.

She's a woman who has a fairly strong denial of psychic reality, a pseudo-mature adjustment, and a very turbulent infantile masturbatory life. She is probably a great masturbator. Has she told you much about it?

MM: No, she hasn't told me.

DM: There is a very rich masturbatory fantasy life and an intense projective identification with you and perhaps other women, as well as representing the maternal figure, and she lives in a kind of vicarious sexuality. And these women have remained friends?

MM: Yes.

DM: Probably the great formative influence in her childhood was being in bed with mummy. She was the only child sleeping upstairs in the house until she was eight, the house meaning also the mother, the geography of the inside of the mother. Does she work as a psychotherapist?

MM: Yes.

DM: Is she tormented by her patients? Because there's a very strong feeling in this dream, in spite of saying they're beautiful rooms, that they really have been ruined by all these people coming in and taking pieces away. And this is what children do to their mothers. They make a wreck of mother. They make her old, exhausted, broken down and, if daddy doesn't continually repair and restore – but he's so busy with his father or his brother that he doesn't restore the mother. This is what children do. And she's worried about whether there is a man in your life restoring you, keeping you healthy and sane, and so on with all these analytic children making a wreck of you. Oh, not her, no, she's a good girl. She wouldn't do that. She pays her taxes. She may be physically ill, but she is in a very hypochondriacal state.

You must remember that in a state of projective identification you have two different types of phenomena. You have the phenomenon of identification: and here it is hypochondriac identification with this exhausted mother, feeling terrible, ruined by the children. On the other hand you have the claustrophobic state of feeling persecuted. Here, the feeling of persecution comes up in the form of the children finding bad food inside the mother and eating it; it is faeces, and they vomit. They make themselves sick, as the bulimics do.

It is a separation phenomenon. The picture is of the child lying in her bed, listening to the noises from the parents' bedroom, masturbating by introducing her fingers into her vagina or her anus, with fantasies of getting inside the mother and wandering about, looking and trying to find out what's happening in there – stealing the food she finds and making herself sick on it.

And this is the situation with the bulimics. They get inside and stuff themselves with mother's faeces and then get sick and vomit. The bulimia goes with the anorexia, because they are frightened that they will gain weight and that everybody will see that they've been stealing food. Any fat feels like faeces under their skin; they feel it is disgusting, like seeing skeletons with fat on them.

At this point, she feels you have no sympathy for her, you are supposed to be the stupid mother with that awful baby – remember the vegetables I gave you yesterday were bad. Maybe because you missed your meal yesterday, on Monday. And you are supposed to know nothing about her masturbation and intruding and stuffing herself with faeces.

This kind of barrier between patient and analyst is very frequently due to the fact that the patient has withheld material from the analyst. So, there is a barrier of secrecy which results in the fact that she can't talk to you because there are so many things she hasn't told you that would enable you to understand her present state and the main thing is the masturbation. And this kind of thing is apt to happen to little girls, daughters and their mothers all the time: that they're ill, they don't feel well, and their mothers are supposed never to suspect that they have been masturbating. Their genitals can be all red, they can have frequency of urination, and itching of the anus, but mothers are never supposed to raise the question that they have been masturbating. This is a secret a mother and daughter collude in keeping.

Daughter and mother are both turning a blind eye to one another's sexuality. Daughter won't ask what mummy does in her bed, and mummy's not supposed to ask what the child does in her bed. So, there is a conspiracy of secrecy in the family about sexuality.

I would have wanted to interpret further that there's a mutual blocking of curiosity. There is a confusion here between secrecy and privacy: she would say that what she does in bed is private too. This dialogue between mother and child: 'But mummy has a right to know.' 'But I have a right to know too!' 'No, you don't have the same right to know about mummy that she has to know about you, because mummy's responsible for you.'

Now: this talk about being drowsy is not an interpretation. It's only outlining the area that needs to be investigated. It has to do with her curiosity about what goes on in the parents' bedroom, and her curiosity about what goes on in your weekend break, your holiday break, and how it is that you seem to survive having all these analytic children who come and rob you and exploit you and leave you exhausted. How do you manage to survive? Her mother didn't survive. How do you manage to survive all these greedy intrusive children? So, what needs to be drawn out specifically in relationship to this material is the hypochondriac state, the claustrophobic state, as manifested by the vomiting.

MM: Here are more sessions:

First session

She arrives eight minutes late. She lies down, sighs, and says she had a dream, but can't remember it very well, just the last part …

I say to the patient, 'I realise you arrived late, and now you're trying to give me something valuable, but in pieces.' (I say it like a neglectful mother who tries to please the daughter who has been waiting for her – an inversion of the relation.)

She keeps silent for about twenty minutes.

'Did what I said affect you that much?' She then says, 'I think you've cut me. You didn't let me tell my dream.'

I then say, 'Why not? I've been waiting in silence for twenty minutes.'

She says, 'But you mentioned my being late, when I intended to talk about something else; you could have mentioned it in the middle or at the end of my speech. You want things your own way.'

I say, 'I think you cannot stand me being free to say what comes out of me, without obeying your schedule: you are the mummy-analyst, and I am the child-patient.'

She answers, 'But it is me who supplies the material here.'

I say, 'Yes, but everything I can see in you is material, and not only what you choose to verbalise. Don't you think so? I don't prevent you from speaking.'

She says, 'And in the dream a delay was implied.'

Session a week later

She arrives eight minutes late. It is a Tuesday, after a holiday Monday. She recounts a dream: '*I was in the small two-storey house where I lived from the age of eleven to seventeen* (until her father sold the bakery). *On the top floor there was a get-together, and I was the age I am now. It was pleasant and when the guests left, I opened a bottle of soda water but, in fact, it was a small bottle of beer, the type for export. I was going to study, but I heard a noise. I went to check. From the top of the stairs, I could see the cupboard door moving. I went down to have a look. There was a man inside it. I ran out of the house scared. Then I woke up, very frightened!*

There were various associations. The patient doesn't like drinking soda water, though she likes beer; later she says she drank beer the day before while she was reading *Faust*. The man in the dream looked like an uncle from Rio. She liked him a lot, and was going to spend her holidays with him. But she liked her cousin (the son of that uncle) even better. He was her idol. He was a newspaper reporter, and she was proud of him. What did she feel in the dream? A threat – of what? She doesn't know at first. Something hidden? I suggest a sexual attack. Her uncle? (says she) – or the father? But she's very far from this idea even in her fantasies. After the beating he had given her, things were never the same again and her father kept away from her as she grew older. Only recently has she become closer and shown some affection for her father. She recalls the fact that her father sold the bakery when she was older. Too many men hung around the place. They meddled with her; she was afraid they would abuse her. She remembers – when she was a young woman – that one of them touched her breasts, pulled down her panties; she was frightened.

While we were talking, I was thinking: here is a double-storey house-personality with a floor upstairs – breasts, food, a get-together of friends with soda water, beer, and ambiguity which had already come up on other occasions such as smoking cigarillos, drinking and being in a state of excitement. This time it was 'the assault' that took place on the lower floor (genitals) with a man hidden, frightening her. What did he want?

I was also thinking of yesterday's session, where nothing happened; it was the 1st of May, a holiday. It is a state of mind which she gets into when she is alone, disturbed by the noise from downstairs made by a hidden man.

DM: She is back inside.

This is a claustrophobic dream. This is the house where she lived during her adolescence. Instead of drinking soda she is drinking beer. Then, she hears a noise as in the first dream, in the first session you brought, when she was ill. In that dream she also hears a noise, and there is a man in the closet. We are back to the parents' intercourse, back inside, stealing food or drinks, and somehow getting drunk and afraid of this father-penis hidden in the closet.

Session ten days later

Louise arrives a few minutes late, and talks about her financial problems. I feel she is very sincere, and realise she is actually going through hard times. She goes on and says that it is difficult to talk about this subject, for she fears it may provoke a catastrophe. She tells me that, at the beginning of the week, she thought about her financial difficulties, but she did not mention them because she felt it was a terrible thing. It could possibly result in her discontinuing her analysis and her analytic training. She asked herself what her role was in these financial troubles. Was she responsible for lots of her patients cancelling their consultations? She is trying to work at her parents' house, in another neighborhood – much farther from the city centre – for it could offer her new job possibilities. But the top price for consultations there was lower. She also tells me that her savings are finished. Her parents agree with her plans, but they are ill and can help her financially only occasionally. And it is hard to ask them for help. Then she starts crying. She says she now knows why she did not want to mention the subject. She recalled how hard it was – as a child – to ask her father for something, such as, to buy a new book for school, to pay for the conservatory fee, etc. Every time she asked for something, her father questioned her. She had a sense of self-devaluation and rejection owing to this characteristic of her father's, but now she understands it was only a foolishness of his.

The way she presented herself at this session was something totally new.

DM: With this desperate tone – because she supposes you're going to say, 'If you can't afford this analysis, go away!'

MM: No, I would never do such a thing!

DM: She is supposing so. Everything is based upon this assumption: if she can't afford it, she must go away. Then, what is the meaning of all this? It is a part of a particular anxiety, a 'toilet anxiety': that is, if you cannot defaecate in the pot, mother is going to throw you into the toilet. It seem that is the fantasy behind it: if you want to have some milk from your mother's breast, you have to pay for it in the pot. And if you get constipated, you'll be flushed down.

MM: But is she presuming she's doing something in order to get constipated?

DM: Are *you* presuming it?

MM: No, she is presuming she must be doing something to provoke her financial difficulty.

DM: Yes, she may be acting her fantasies, treating the analyst as if she were saying, 'You either pay, or go away'; but she may also be enacting such fantasies with her father, looking for ways to antagonise him and pushing him to say no. This must be investigated, but the main point is that you would be that 'business mummy' who would say, 'If there's no money, there's no analysis'. Now this, of course, is a great defence of hers against feeling grateful and experiencing you as a generous person.

Final considerations

From the material presented to him, Meltzer saw Louise as a manic-depressive personality, with homosexual tendencies. In his article 'A contribution to the metapsychology of cyclothymic states' (1963), using clinical material from a five-year analysis, he details the psychic structure of the manic-depressive state as one in which the breast-penis is stolen and projected into the father's penis, which becomes an idealised object of oral greed, leaving the breast vulnerable to attack. Such a tendency leads to instability in sexual identifications, as well as to a confusion between male and female.

In another of Louise's dreams six months after the narrative presented to Meltzer for supervision there appeared an image equivalent to the penis-scrotum object: *a Chianti red-wine bottle; also a breast-desk with two drawers whose sphincter-nipples were removed; and afterwards in the dream she is at a wild feast with these nipple-penis Chianti red-wine bottles.* The dream occurred after I had had to cancel the previous session (a Thursday), and when I told her in advance during the Wednesday session, she could not come up with an alternative date. At the time I felt her disguised hostility, but it was not possible to talk to her about it because she withdrew into a suppressed silence that in previous sessions she described as a 'drowsiness state' in which she hears but feels absent-minded and is not able to answer.

On the following Monday, she came in cheerfully, on time, and said it seemed a long time since she was last here. After that she related a dream she had the night before, saying that she thought that the colours in the dream were important (only now has she noticed that hers are colour dreams; probably this had been happening even before she started analysis): *There was a war atmosphere; they seemed German or Italian, fleeing from the war. There were a lot of people. I was young and my father was there, perhaps my whole family, and we came to a place where we were going to stay. There was this room that was going to be mine, finally a place for me to stay, with a beautiful desk of a red-wine colour, English style, big, with two small drawers that could be locked like a safe; there was a safe code.* (Later she added that the drawers were open and that she had always wanted such a desk.) *But then we had to go away, we are getting on a train or bus, perhaps a large wagon train, with a lot of people. There were men in uniform; they looked Italian, with dark blue uniforms with white stripes or white round spots, perhaps it was the ticket controller. They joined the train driver for a photo and when I saw them together for the picture I found it funny, they seemed like clown; the atmosphere was Italian. There was also another scene that I don't remember well, with Chianti wine, that bottle covered with straw.*

I thought, here is something in common – red wine in the bottle, and the desk was the colour of red wine. The patient's associations were that German or Italian refers to the analyst; she felt anxious in the dream scene when she had to escape; she found the photo-taking scene and the Chianti red wine good and amusing. I associate the dream to the events on Wednesday's session: the war atmosphere, the silence, and the escapist atmosphere when she 'withdrew' into her drowsiness incommunicability. The dream began with a threat from which she had to flee and that became something good and funny by the end of the dream, like what she did at the end of Wednesday's session when she took her leave saying 'see you tomorrow' although she knew that I was not going to see her.

The first part of the dream conveys emotions of hostility owing to the expulsion, a sense of displacement until a place is found with something long-desired – the desk-breast, the original breast object now the analytical breast. But this place has to be abandoned and she is compelled to get on a large wagon-train where the atmosphere is a festive gathering with wine and clown-men – indicating with disdain her passage from the breast to the penis. This is what the red-wine colour dream image seems to indicate, with its part-object little desk-drawers and Chianti bottle, breast and penis. The analyst-breast-desk is lost and she yields to a bottle-penis that puts her in the midst of a wild feast, pointing to her manic-depressive states due to the pre-genital oedipal organisation that keeps her in a level of poor symbolisation.

On the transference level the patient seems to have had an emotional experience that she could not digest (when I told her about the cancellation): she withdrew from contact, invoking drowsiness, not answering my words, and when the session came to an end she pretended our usual session was going to take place the next day. Her reaction to the session's postponement can be seen in the two little drawers that were lockable but in the dream were open, equivalent to a breast whose sphincter-nipples have been removed. It is possible to speculate that she felt dislodged from her place, excluded by the analyst who was filling her time with something else, and she felt the cancellation as equivalent to being expelled from the parents' room due to the arrival of somebody else (a primal scene).

Three years later, she discontinued analysis. By that time she had reached some understanding of her emotional states which she previously regarded as physical diseases. She had acquired some capacity to turn emotional impulses into symbolic elements. She frequently felt responsible for her mental states. As I see it, it was the beginning of genuine reparation, but it needed more analysis for this process to be complete, in order to work through her oedipal tendencies and the pain of the depressive anxieties that appeared in her sessions from this time until she stopped analysis.

CHAPTER TWO

On the trail of of voyeurism
(1996)

Célia Fix Korbivcher

Cristina is a 25-year-old woman who has been in analysis with me for some years. Originally she came three times a week, but last year we moved up to four sessions a week at my suggestion. She is single, and her parents are separated. There is more information about her history, but I should perhaps leave it for later.

Donald Meltzer: Yes. Let's see the clinical material.

Célia Korbivcher: This session happened on a Friday and was a replacement for the Monday session. It was the first week of analysis after the holidays. We had agreed to this replacement session before the holidays because I was going to resume working on Tuesday.

DM: Then, it is a replacement session for the previous Monday.

CK: Yes. When Cristina arrived, she said that she almost did not show up that day because she had forgotten. She said: 'I suddenly opened my appointment book and saw the appointment there. Then, I called to confirm and decided not even to go to work in the afternoon.' She sighs and in an enthusiastic tone, says: 'I didn't sit down the whole day. Let's see what will happen. It is good to do so much; this prevents me from getting depressed.' In the previous sessions, the atmosphere was what she calls depressive. She continued to talk about her work.

DM: What type of work is it?

CK: Cristina is a design artist, she works on illustrations for covers of notebooks, appointment books, and calendars based on her own work. The motifs vary; some were extracted from artistic photos that she took.

She continues with her report, mentioning that she has to take care of packing and has a lot to do. She soon interrupts and says: 'Today I again had the same dream. *I dreamed of a man, another man who looks like John*' (mentioning a man much older than her, with whom she had a brief romance). '*I was in a bar – a place with many men – naked, seducing them all, but I was feeling awful about everything.*'

DM: Weren't the men naked?

CK: No, it was only her. '*Then Pedro and Vera appeared*' (a couple of friends whom she often talks about) '*and covered me with a jacket and took me away.*'

DM: Did this happen in a bar or in a swimming pool?

CK: In a bar. She continued: 'And I thought that I was calmer lately. My friend (a man with whom she works) mentioned this weekend that I was flirting a lot.'

DM: Is he a sexual partner?

CK: No. Cristina went on: 'I flirted with so and so – I didn't even notice.' I tell her that what draws my attention is that she is unable to stop because she has to avoid becoming depressed. 'You have to take many steps. In your dream, when you appear naked, it suggests to me a situation of helplessness and not a sexual situation. You think that if you flirt you will get everything you need.'

DM: This is a good interpretation that tries to establish a differentiation between her being naked defensively or seductively. Because in the dream, Pedro and Vera throw a jacket to protect her. Then, she seems to listen to what her colleague says about her not being aware of her seductive behaviour. Of course, this does not mean that it must necessarily be one thing or another, seduction or vulnerability. It can be both.

CK: Cristina pauses for a long time, and moments later says that she was thinking about her work, the tasks scheduled for that day. She lists several of her activities. I tell her that, in fact, as she had mentioned in the beginning, 'You cannot stop, otherwise you will become depressed. We were talking about something close to you, and you quickly interrupted and replaced it with all these tasks. It is possible that the numerous affairs, men, and dates may not be any different, may not express a genuine interest in any partner.'

DM: This activity of taking pictures, these appointment books, and the dream in which she is seductive with men in the bar, suggest a situation of projective identification inside her mother's vagina, with penises all around, with several men entering successively inside this mother. This suggests a reference to the holidays, the change in the day of the session, and things that may be going on in the transference. Perhaps a prostituted analyst.

CK: Continuing, she says: 'It is true. Today I caused a lot of confusion.' She says that she gathered a large number of people for a certain programme that night. 'It seems I had to gather all my friends so it would not look like I was arriving alone at this place.' Her communication is quite long and detailed, and she names the friends and the location. The programme consists of their dancing at a friend's bar, and there was a certain atmosphere connected to the event at the bar.

DM: She seems to be in a type of nymphomaniac mania, requiring what the Germans call *Gupersech*.

CK: I tell her that the confusion that she caused was actually here in the analysis. 'You created confusion with all these people, perhaps as a way of not staying in the situation here.' At that moment, it seems that she becomes aware of what I am communicating to her. Then, I bring up the dream again, saying that the image of the naked woman among all those men is more her need of being someone interesting and the target of all the attention, so she can feel that she exists and is someone. It reminded me of an image (and I may have told her that) of a small child who needs to be the object of all the adults' attention.

DM: I think it is important to interpret the transference in the context of an infant's transference: that she is a little girl in an adults' party, and starts to take off her clothes to draw attention. This line of interpretation, that such mania is a form of defence against the analytical situation, is doubtful because it may in fact be a demonstration of exactly the way she is involved in the analytical situation: that she is very excited to be back in this prostituted mother's vagina.

CK: I said: 'It seems you don't feel you have inside yourself something that gives you the idea that you exist. So you set up a series of confusing situations, involving people, exposing yourself, making yourself the object of everyone's attention so you can feel that you have an autonomous existence. In fact, the couple in your dream who appear and cover you are protecting you. I think this is related to some perception on your part that the conversation here helps to take care of you.

And Cristina says: 'Yes, I do just that,' referring to the confusion.

DM: She is a patient who feels good by setting up social confusion because she is a mentally confused person. But this state leads to group formation because it is more comfortable to be confused in a group than by herself, alone.

CK: Then, she starts to report the following situation: owing to intervention by her partner, a supplier became more flexible in a work negotiation. She and the partner had gone to discuss a work matter, but the person was not willing to meet some of their requests. During the conversation, the partner realised he had common interests with this person. They then had a long chat, and the supplier gradually became interested in both of them and they came to an agreement that suited them both.

DM: They found a common symbolism.

CK: She says: 'That happened naturally.' She makes a comparison between her own attitude and that of her friend. 'I am not like him. Before long I try to seduce to get what I want.' She is astonished to realise that it could be different.

DM: It seems that she is saying: my friend is interested in finding this common symbolism, but I go straight to the penis.

CK: I say that perhaps she felt that our conversation also had this quality, and now she may feel more at ease, without having to take so many steps to avoid feeling threatened.

DM: Perhaps it is true that she is feeling more comfortable with you, because you are like the friend, you are interested in the symbolism and are not excited about all the penises that are out there.

CK: At this moment, Cristina mentions that she remembered one of her works, which had a picture with a form suggestive of a happy little clown who seemed to be dancing. She then says in a more depressed tone: 'I remember one of the images which seemed to show a man clutching onto another in order not to sink.'

DM: A famous English poet [Stevie Davies] wrote: 'I was much too far out all my life, and not waving but drowning': I was asking for help – which shows this oscillation between mania and claustrophobia in a depression.

CK: I said, 'Your tone of voice is more depressed. You seem, in fact, to be in touch with what we were talking about at that moment.' I tell her that the images that she brings with this recollection seem to synthesise our conversation: 'It is possible that this image of a man clutching a person to avoid sinking is close to how you really feel. The image of the little clown contrasts with it.' I tell her something about the little clown having the function of preventing depression. 'It seems that today we can talk about all this. I think that the men may have the function of something you can clutch in order to feel you are somebody. As I said in the beginning, it is possible that your recollection of the appointment and the cancellation of your work so you could come here may have occurred because this experience is different from all the acting-out in which you have been involved. Here you can think, and not just repeat it all, as you have been doing for a long time.'

DM: I think that this is a good interpretation that contains the oscillation between mania and depression and raises questions about this commercial activity, as to whether it is not in essence acting out. It is difficult not to feel that something very pornographic emerges from this activity of taking photos.

CK: I would like to make a comment. The analysis is paid for by her father, and she claims she has some financial problems. Lately, this patient's work has been very slow. She has constant complaints that it is not changing, that it is not developing. Despite her financial challenges, I proposed adding a fourth session and suggested that she could perhaps arrange to pay for this fourth session. Her work comes a little within this financial context.

DM: The financial difficulties are linked to the father's financial difficulties?

CK: Yes.

DM: This is what she says. When amid that sort of slow situation you propose to her to start a fourth session and to pay herself with some sort of work, you are behaving in a manner that probably suggests that you do not believe she is having financial difficulties.

This position seems quite precarious and can place her in a mercenary light, as if you were asking her to go on the streets, which can contribute to the type of transference in which you are a mother-prostitute. Care is required when dealing with money issues in an analysis. If you believed that there are indeed financial difficulties with the father, I do not understand why you did not insist on her paying for one of the three existing sessions. But why did you request a fourth session?

CK: As an attempt to create better conditions so the work could perhaps develop. It was very slow and with her constant complaints a vicious circle was formed.

DM: It is difficult to see the logic of this. I can believe that the work was revitalised, but I am not sure that it was in a good way. It is a situation that lends itself to projective identifications. How did her friend join the partnership?

CK: I cannot specify; it was a casual situation. Cristina is surprised that for the first time she is able to have a non-romantic relationship with a friend.

DM: Did she have a sexual relationship with him?

CK: No. I would like to mention another fact: the patient always speaks of her mother as someone excessively sexual in her behaviour.

DM: Then, now we have the set-up for the photos: it is voyeurism of the relationship of the mother with the various penises, her incipient sexual relationship with the penis. A person who lives in projective identification, even if it is only in the sexual area, who is in a projective identification with the mother's vagina, with the mother's sexuality, must bring into the transference the acting-out of this situation, which is fundamentally nymphomaniac, if it is to replace this manic quality by the claustrophobic anguish of drowning. Therefore, the acting-out within the transference must be brought closer to the outside situation to be able to reveal the nature of the transference. What we have up till now is that for the patient, the mother is like a nymphomaniac with whom she dreams all the time. But with you, it seems that the balance is tending towards the claustrophobia of drowning.

The way you deal with the frequency and payment of the extra session will influence the balance between the acting-in and acting-out. If an analyst suggests increasing the frequency of the sessions to a patient in financial difficulties this will make the patient feel that it is backed by a financial interest.

As you were finding the analysis was somehow stuck, you believed that a fourth session could help. What you can do in a situation like this is, for example, to agree on a weekly amount instead of payment per session, and let the amount be divided by the number of sessions you deem necessary. This movement of changing from fees per session to weekly fees, decreasing the amount for each session, motivates the patient to help pay in some way, without you stepping into the role of someone who says: 'Look, you are a nymphomaniac. I think you should start making money with this.'

CK: I wanted to discuss precisely this because I had many doubts about this issue.

DM: Let's move on to the next bit.

CK: This session occurred a week after the session previously narrated. Cristina says: 'My father has not provided the payment. I have already asked several times, but he has not left the cheque.' I ask: 'What do you think about this?' She says: 'I should have been more committed. I think I am like this because it is expensive, and I have been coming for ages, and it is a waste of time. Like yesterday, when I was sleepy and nothing happened. On the other hand, I thought, my mother is travelling and I am taking care of my own affairs; I am well. When I left the car, coming here, I thought: it will be just the same, I have nothing useful to say.'

DM: Is this heavy atmosphere usual?

CK: Yes, the atmosphere is usually heavy. There seems to be something aggressive in her communication. I say: 'From your point of view, yesterday's session was a waste of time. This is how you transformed what we talked about. I remember that we talked about your wish to be involved only in successful situations, ignoring unpleasant ones.'

I add that today is another session, a different session, that does not need to repeat that. She pauses for a long time. I tell her that I observe the conversation has been interrupted.

After the silence, Cristina mentions that yesterday she told her friend, regarding her ex-boyfriend, that it was not good to be sad because of him, it was better to go dancing. I say she expects me to make the connections that she does not make. For example, to realise that she did not manage to make the payment like she wanted brought her some sadness and depression, perhaps because she could not be the person she would like to be. She pauses again and says that she was thinking about the university and what she talked about yesterday. She pauses again for a long time.

I observe a huge distance, shutdown, disinterest, lack of curiosity. She says: 'Yesterday, I was with my friend and we smoked. I smoked three cigarettes and told her that smoking is better than kissing.' She mentions that she said this because she did not know what to say, even though she thought about not saying it. I say that when she talks about 'kissing', I suppose that she is kissing a living being, who would have a real presence in the situation, which could stimulate a variety of reactions, such as enjoyment and frustration; whereas the cigarette is only a cigarette, an object that she uses and throws away: 'It seems that this describes precisely the experience of this session: you try to remove the life, the interest of the encounter, to avoid the suffering and pain. As at the beginning, you become isolated, grumbling, say that it is expensive and is no use for anything and only makes you sleepy.' She pauses; the conversation seems disjointed. She then says: 'Yesterday I thought about two of the works I like most: one was the one that I gave you, inspired by a specific situation; and there is another one. The trouble is they were not my creations but someone else's.'

I tell her that this is what results from our conversation, which keeps coming to nothing, and this was also the fate of our session yesterday. She then comments that a friend, who works with *papier-mâché* sculptures of dolls, came to her house. And, at night, she dreamed that she was in a place where there was a display window with sculptures of steel and everything was very beautiful. She describes the metalwork in rich detail. I say: 'The dream is yours, it is your product, it comes from inside you and not from your friend. You don't seem to realise that you have inside yourself the possibility of creating.'

DM: This does not take into consideration that this is perhaps a *voyeuristic* behaviour that happens through a window, and this is probably the nature of her creativity, which would correspond to the activity of taking photographs. Then, although she complains that nothing happens in the sessions, she recognises in the dream that you are very creative and artistic, but she deals with this in the same way as the cigarettes. She does not receive your interpretation as if it were a kiss between her and you, like a baby kissing the mother's breast. She treats it as a cigarette that she sucks and throws away. I think that this dream reveals a lot about the nature of the situation. And that the financial situation is indeed a smokescreen for the emotional situation. It is interesting that her creativity is represented by sculptures made of steel, which is a durable material, and not of *papier-mâché*, which needs to be built up.

Participant: The dream seems to be about her mother, with whom she lives in projective identification, and perhaps she would not have the same thing with the analyst.

DM: It seems unlikely that the photography could be on an equal footing with the sculpture in terms of creativity. Some artists combine photography and sculpture, photography and painting, but I think that the work of the analyst does not mix with that of the photographer, even if we take into account that the work of the analyst is fundamentally descriptive. The description involves a degree of transformation, to the extent that the analyst comprehends the meaning of the symbolic formation and, in some situations, transforms the symbol, acting as alpha function for the patient. I do not think that this is the type of patient for whom the analyst performs alpha function, but certainly some manic patients continue the hyperactivity of children with defective symbol formation. I don't see defective symbol formation in this patient; what I see more is the concreteness of the symbol-formation owing to projective identification.

Participant: Does a defect in symbol formation precede difficulties arising from the use of projective identification?

DM: Defects in the formation of fundamental symbols and in the ability to form symbols certainly have their origins in a remote time in the child's life and leave deep scars. On the other hand, some defects in symbol formation contribute to the situation in which emotional experiences are transformed into psychosomatic phenomena due to the lack of symbols that would allow their mentalisation. But this patient does not seem to make transformations of psychosomatic phenomena. She rather seems a manic personality who is constantly in projective identification with her mother's vagina – a mother seen by her as promiscuous – and probably with a father whom she feels as sexual and erotic.

I think that the problem is in coming out of projective identification. At the moment, this shows itself in oscillating waves of manic exhibitionism and drowning. Here she smokes cigarettes enjoying the idea that she can throw them away, by contrast with kissing the person she is with – evidence of the creative capacity of producing babies.

The sculptures in the dream probably represent other patients of the analyst, people whom she has met or heard about, who do not seem to be so stuck in their analyses. We do not hear much about this, but one must be attentive to encounters between patients.

Let's continue.

CK: Cristina is very moved, cries in silence, she is in fact quite touched. I tell her that in this session we see that 'if you are in touch with what goes on inside you, then you feel moved and become depressed. You want to avoid the pain and sadness, and this results in this situation of depletion.'

DM: This is probably true, but not unequivocally true, because the analyst has interpreted the sculptures as the analysand's own production, and not as *voyeurism* of the analyst's creativity. It is momentarily comforting to the patient, but she does not in fact believe that.

The patient says that she does not feel creative, that everything she does comes from the creativity of others. This is also ambiguous, because all creative people argue the same thing, which is, that the creativity is not theirs but comes from inspiration, which Milton expressed when saying that his poetry did not come to him on demand, it came from his muse. In fact, in his blindness, it came in a dream, and was dictated during sleep. A talented novelist dreamed that he used to sit on a stool wearing headphones and writing everything that was dictated through the headphones.

You may be able to take her out of the state she is in, I do not think that it is very deep. It is constructed from the fact that she has a poor opinion of her own mother – which you do not necessarily need to share – but it is also built around a very intrusive voyeurism, probably aggravated by your holidays, such nice holidays that you could not manage to be back on Monday. This probably raises serious suspicions. But she is a good girl. I think she is relatively unsophisticated, but is intelligent and sensitive, and has had an unlucky upbringing.

CK: The question of creativity is a wide one. There was a lot of pain when she realised the feeling of inner emptiness. She says that everything that she produces is only an imitation. In the dream, she refers to the dolls as little dolls.

DM: I saw that in the offices here there are many works of art, beautiful objects. I would ask what specifically she saw in your consulting room.

CK: Not exactly art objects, but in front of the couch there is a closed bookcase, a type of a showcase with books inside.

DM: It seems obvious to me that she is impressed with your analytical skills, but does not know how to use them. I think the problem is that she seems to oscillate between mania and depression and does not know how to get out of her projective identification.

Participant: I would like to ask whether the patient's artistic activity or her use of this capacity would be predominantly an acting-out or some type of sublimation.

DM: I do not see anything as sublimation. I do not find a place, in my way of thinking, for the concept of sublimation. I think it is important to differentiate between 'acting-out' and 'acting-in' in the transference, because it allows you to outline the emotional elements within the transference situation, in which there are more possibilities of modification, not only by the interpretation but also by the state of mind and behaviour of the analyst.

Participant: How would you explain the identification of projection into her mother's vagina? In your work *Dream Life* you spoke about the importance of projective identification in the interpretation of dreams and in the clinical discussions. That made sense to me, but now I am lost.

DM: I regret that the book *The Claustrum* has not yet been translated into Portuguese. In this book I describe how the states of projective identification are fundamentally states of projective identification with the mother as internal object and, depending on the intention of the intrusion and the reasons for being in projective identification, the parts of the personality that are projected go either to the rectum, genital, or head-breast. The phenomenology of projective identification is different according to each of these areas of the mother's body. The identification with the inside of the rectum is associated with perversion and sadomasochism. The identification with the inside of the vagina connects to an area of erotomania and grandiosity, whereas the identification with the inside of the breast or head produces a different phenomenology, a type of complacency, indolence, and omniscience. In the book I refer to an overwhelmingly complacent character called Oblomov in the Russian novel by Goncharov – a baby at the breast.

Participant: I would like to ask why there are only three of these models. Can't the projective identification be with the father's penis?

DM: The entrance doors of projective identification correspond primarily to holes in the mother's body. It is true that there are ears, eyes, nostrils, etc. But those are the three main doors. If you want to rob a bank, you can enter from the floor or roof, breaking in somehow but, in general, you enter through the doors. I remember a French movie about a bank robbery that was conducted through the sewer. The thieves arrived through the sewage pipes and went inside the safe through the floor, stole everything and left through the sewage again. Projective identification in the rectum and anus always has the intention of making the journey all the way to the breast from the inside. But we also see the opposite, which would be projective identification with the breast making a tortuous course downwards to the vagina or to the rectum.

Many of these phenomena are present in the descriptions that Melanie Klein makes of the old paranoid-schizoid position, before the role of projective identification was understood and the reasons for stealing from the inside of the mother's body were clearly seen by Mrs Klein.

Participant: I was thinking about everything that has been said here today, about how to approach the clinical material of this patient, and it seems to me that your way would be to begin from a rather more primitive or lower level than the one that I, for example, work with.

DM: It may be deep, but is not necessarily primitive. What I am suggesting is that you go after her trail of voyeurism, because this will give access to various pathways, for example, group sex, money, greed – or what she believes to be greed for money – leading to issues such as envy, creativity, babies, etc. If you stay attentive to the signs of voyeurism, this may lead you to all these other transformations.

CHAPTER THREE

Emergence from living in projective identification
(1996)

Martha Maria de Moraes Ribeiro

Elisa is a 46-year-old woman who has been in analysis for almost eight years, with four sessions a week, during which she has tried to emerge from an archaic defensive system which I will refer to as a prey–predator relationship.

Donald Meltzer: Could you explain to me why you have chosen this term instead of the ordinary term sadomasochism?

Martha Ribeiro: This has to do with the patient's history. She is a researcher working in the field of prey–predation relationships and tonic immobility.

DM: In what? In what sense, predation?

MR: I will explain. Elisa was originally referred to me by G, who shortly after died. After her friend's death, her somatisations gained strength again, with diarrhoea and abdominal cramps, and her depression worsened to such an extent that her creative, concentrating, and working capacities were becoming paralysed. She was afraid of not being able to continue with her work as a professor at the university.

DM: So G was her girlfriend?

MR: Yes. When she first came to me for analysis Elisa walked with a stiff posture and when she greeted me, she wouldn't move her hands; her look was timid and she hardly ever looked straight at me. She would lie motionless on the couch, always wearing the same clothes, and her voice seemed to echo out from her stiff body, denoting a mental state of immobility.

During the initial interview, she told me her father was born in Germany and is 76 years old. He is a retired industrialist and has always been a strict and stern man. Her mother was born in Belgium and had always been very ill, with deep, recurrent depressions that rendered her psychically absent for long periods. When she was pregnant with Elisa, she discovered that her husband had a mistress, which increased her depression and the hopelessness she felt towards life. She passed away nine years ago on her second suicide attempt, when she took a lethal dose of an agrochemical and tranquillisers. Elisa has two siblings, a brother who is six years older than her and a sister four years younger.

When she decided to study medicine, she left home for the first time and began a relationship with a man 20 years older than her, with whom she had her first heterosexual experiences. He had an athletic body and, like herself, was a nature-lover. After one year in this relationship, he died from bronchopneumonia. After graduating from medical school, she decided to become a researcher and got a position at the university where she works, moving away from her family. Her first homosexual relationships began at this time. She had three lovers, the first being G, with whom she had a relationship for seventeen years. The second was H, also a researcher, with whom she stayed for three years; and her third and current partner is N, a psychologist living in another state. G died from cancer when Elisa was starting her relationship with H, who also had breast cancer when she decided to leave her to stay with N.

Elisa feels she has tragically destructive forces within her that were exacerbated by experiences of loss in her relationships with her early objects. Thus, she feels herself to be a great predator who goes through life immobilising and killing her prey; those who live close to her are bound to fall sick, to die, and to abandon her. External reality seemed to her to confirm her theories and nurtured within her an omnipotent belief in her destructive feelings.

As a researcher in the field of neurophysiology, Elisa has a special talent for reporting her scientific work. Early in her treatment she described a study of hers that contained a meaningful metaphor about her own mental functioning: to living beings, she argued, immobility is a guarantee of survival and movement is a threat to life.

She then came up with the following information:

'I am preparing a conference for the national conference on ethology, and the topic I was invited to talk about is tonic immobility and animal hypnosis. While reviewing my data, I found something that made me feel excited: tonic immobility is a defensive reaction or a reversible state of inactivity observed in several groups of vertebrate and invertebrate animals. This had already been noted by Darwin. Scientists regard tonic immobility as the last stage in a sequence of responses that occur in the confrontation between prey and predator; it would be a last resource of the prey in an attempt to fool its predator. Many experiments show that unmoving animals are less prone to be predated upon and, therefore, this would be a valuable survival strategy. This phenomenon is also sometimes described as animal hypnosis, which is inaccurate because there is a close relationship between tonic immobility and fear, which excludes any resemblance to human hypnosis, in which cooperation between the hypnotiser and the hypnotised is an essential feature. But what I found is that there is a bridge between tonic immobility and the modulation of pain. So, in one of my investigations, I found that when I stimulated a certain region of the animal's brain with acetylcholine, I was able to inhibit not only movement, but also the reflex to painful stimuli for a period of one hour (immobilisation lasts for fifteen minutes). The practical application of this is that if the animal is bitten, it will remain immovable, because if it felt pain while being attacked, it would move and the predator would go on to eat it. Thus, two factors contribute to preserve animal life: immobility in the face of the aggressor (playing dead) and the absence of pain for a period of one hour.

I discovered this this morning and I had to tell these discoveries to someone.'

DM: It's really hot out of the press! Continue.

MR: From the beginning, I felt that I was facing a person with a higher intelligence, but whose emotional development had been halted in the early days of her existence.

I hypothesised that Elisa had suffered a major loss when her psychic apparatus was still unable to replace the loss of a concrete object with symbolisation. As a consequence, she has a fragile psychic organisation, with an enduring and tragic expectation of being abandoned by her objects, which turns her into a victim or prey. Using the biological model, Elisa found a way to intercept pain between two beings. In the analytical relationship, as she is initially unable to introject her analyst as an adequate object, but only as a threatening one, Elisa tries to evade the pain that emerges in transference through the repetition of painful experiences, acting-out through her speech. In this game, she uses language to become either a predator or prey, trying to immobilise the analyst and paralyse the analytical process.

Through words, she becomes a predator and I am turned into her prey, as can be seen when her speech is filled with rich metaphors and analogies, or lengthy and intellectualised, or when she acts in a hostile way, raising doubts about the analytical method. She can also become prey herself when she turns me into a predator as I try hard to decode her comments; she then becomes fragile, keeps silent for long periods, and closes herself in her retreat.

DM: That's a very interesting story, really. I mean, one is inclined to say: 'Bad luck old girl.' But she won't have that. She wants to invest these losses with significance – to take them as evidence of her omnipotence.

MR: That's right. In one of the sessions we will see that she grows bigger when someone dies.

DM: Now, there's something I feel I want to know. This first love of hers, was he the only heterosexual lover she's had?

MR: He was.

DM: And these two homosexual lovers – the one who died and the other one who has breast cancer – did she actually abandon them in favour of a new lover? Or did she carry on both relationships simultaneously?

MR: She was getting emotionally involved with the second lover when the first one got sick, and later she was getting involved with the third lover when the disease appeared in the second one.

DM: That doesn't answer my question. Did she carry on the sexual relationship with one at time or did she carry on with two at a time?

MR: One at a time.

DM: One at a time, right. I'm trying to understand a little more about what it is that she's so excited about this morning that she has to communicate it immediately. She feels she has discovered the two factors that preserve the animal's life: immobility in the face of the aggressor and absence of pain for a period of an hour. And that period of the hour seems to be critical. I presume that is the statement about the transference. One could probably read 50 minutes for the hour. Now, there's no doubt that she has succeeded in interesting you greatly.

MR: She is very seductive.

DM: And, in a sense, she is offering you also an alternative to psychoanalysis for understanding her. I asked whether she carried on two love affairs at the same time because she seems to be carrying on these two love affairs with her research and her analysis at the same time. It still isn't clear to me what was the urgency to communicate this to someone, and why you are the someone. Is it clear why she needed to tell someone about these discoveries?

MR: I think so. She needed someone, but it was a someone that still had no representation inside her.

DM: What was the urgency?

MR: I don't know.

DM: No, you don't know; I don't know either. And it was probably that she felt that somehow her devices of immobility and neutralisation of pain for an hour were being threatened and that she was on the verge of experiencing terrible pain. Okay. Let's go on.

MR: I made a summary of the story of her analysis. It is a long story so I have divided it into three phases, but in fact these three phases overlap.

Phase One (about one year): For quite some time the analysis developed in a favourable setting. Using rich language, the patient gradually described the catastrophic experiences she had been through early in life, in a time when she was still unable to psychically contain or work through what she felt. Elisa seemed to have found her lost object, the lack of which had triggered all her symptoms. She would come to all her sessions, was seldom late, her symptoms had improved, her scientific production was also doing well, and she had been elected chair of the department where she works.

DM: Now, let's get the chronology a little clearer. At the time she started her analysis with you, was she already having her relationship with the fellow who died of bronchopneumonia?

MR: No, it was much later. She was in her second homosexual relationship and about to start the third one when she came to analysis.

Phase Two: The countertransference seemed to indicate that her analysis was about to become paralysed. There were moments in which I would feel my thinking was immobilised. She would listen attentively to me, but would not respond directly to my interpretations. Her utterances had the function of preventing me from getting in contact with her or, much of the time, I would feel engulfed, petrified. In this phase, her defences had reached their apex; I understood she had a need to keep me away from her so that she would not revive in the transference the threat of catastrophe she felt had occurred with her earlier objects. This phase lasted for around a year and a half.

Phase Three: Breaches begin to occur in her defences and there are moments of intimacy in the analytical relationship. These first took place in dreams; then she started to say more directly that she was willing to open up the encapsulated part inside her and Elisa was able, for the first time, to cry with her analyst during the session.

I have three sessions to illustrate these phases.

DM: And how long was Phase Three?

MR: The phases are mixed up to the present.

DM: Up to the present, right. Let's say five and a half years? Now, where is homosexual lover three in relation to these phases?

MR: She has been present from the beginning of the analysis.

DM: At this point of transition from number two to number three homosexual lover, right?

MR: Yes.

DM: Well, it's important to work this out because she has a omnipotent, omniscient certainty about her destructive effect on these people. So it looks as if keeping her distance from you is a technique for keeping you alive. So that her urgency to tell you about this – this discovery of hers – was not only an urgency because of an impending threat to her life but, at the same time, an impending threat to your life, because this prey–predator thing is very reversible. Now, it's still not clear to me why we should call it prey–predator instead of sadomasochistic. I mean, it looks like sadomasochism plus omnipotence. Her mother committed suicide when she was how old?

MR: Eight years ago, when she was around 38 years old.

DM: And the mother was how old? Do you know?

MR: I don't remember, but probably between 60 and 70.

DM: Right, okay. Now, clinical material. Phase One.

MR: Phase One. In one of her first sessions, Elisa brings up a metaphor for her biological birth. She arrives for her session, the fourth of the week, lies on the couch, and starts speaking without interruption: 'Yesterday, if I had had to stay here after your interpretation at the end of the session, I wouldn't have tolerated it.'

DM: Warning. The warning light has gone on.

MR: 'Something has immobilised you', I say. And she says: 'It has to do with what we talked about, the intrauterine condition. The womb should be a place of ideal comfort, with no hunger, no thirst, no pain, and no cold; after we are born, we need to cry and cry in order to survive. Then I remembered two facts which I learned from my mother. The first was when I was born. They said I cried a lot, that I cried so much in my first days that my parents shut me away in a dark room, and then I stopped crying.

I was always a kind child, according to their picture. My mother said she had done this because my father could not miss a night of sleep, he had to work the next day and the children could not make a noise.

'I started early to silence my emotions. My mother would recall this fact whenever she was expressing her views about how to raise children. The second similar thing that happened to me was when I climbed a tree, fell down, broke my arm, and had to have a cast put on it. At night, after the cast was on, I felt too much pain and cried a lot. My mother got up and reproached me, saying that I had to stop crying so I wouldn't disturb my father's sleep. From then on I caused no more worries; they always thought I was a model child, who would not do anything wrong and was always quiet.'

She goes on associating that throughout her life she had tried to solve all her problems on her own, by contrast with her brother, who was rebellious and problematic.

DM: The warning that she gave you in the beginning of this session now turns out to be a warning that she will stop complaining, that she will become immobilised, silent, a perfect child, because the alternatives are either to disturb daddy's sleep and interfere with his work, or to drive mother to suicide. And it seems quite clear that if you are going to talk about her intrauterine life in a way that causes her pain, you're going to be treated with this silence: treatment that will drive you mad. Now, personally, I wouldn't see any necessity for believing the so-called facts about her childhood and development and so on. They simply seem to be techniques for threatening you, and threatening you in a particular way that claims historical precedent. Now, in claiming historical precedent, she also probably denies any responsibility or choice. It's called solving her problems alone.

MR: It seems that's how it worked for a long time. During this phase, this was the situation with me in her analysis.

DM: Right. And we can assume that this confrontation was about seven years ago, is that right?

MR: Yes. After that she paused, and I say that, by bringing up these memories, she is trying to tell me that she has survived and that in order to survive one must cry. And there she was with me, and I could hear her crying. She became afraid of my closeness, paused, and sobbing and stirred, says that she had not found her space in her family, that she had never caused trouble to her parents, had always been kind and had good grades at school. At work, with her colleagues and subordinates, she always tried to do everything that was asked of her, yet was unable to assert herself, and always felt exploited.

DM: Exploited?

MR: Yes. Now she was able to speak more calmly and I said: 'When you need to assert yourself, you are afraid that your words and your crying will break people down, that your words might destroy the others. Then you become silent, as if you didn't exist.'

Elisa says: 'I feel that I block strong emotions. When my mother died and when G died I didn't seem to care at the time; it came later. I still can't do anything with G's house, which shares a wall with mine, as her presence is so strong. I can't go to BA [Buenos Aires] for a visit because she is buried there. When she died I faced it all, I went all the way to Guarulhos Airport to ship her body, but I couldn't attend her funeral.'

I say to her: 'Behind the girl who won't cry and who apparently doesn't feel anything, there's someone who feels a lot and who comes to show her pain to me. Today you are here with your wound exposed, as you were when you were a little girl under that tree you fell from and nobody caught you. Today you are not as lonely as you were then.'

She replies: 'I wanted an explanation for all this difficulty that I have in showing my feelings. I have always thought of it as a matter of race. My father was German and my mother Belgian; I think it's all the same thing. I've stayed single, but my brother and sister married Brazilians and this must have smoothed it over.'

I say: 'And you came for analysis with a Brazilian and here you try to soothe your pain, or at least to get to know it.'

DM: What is this business about G's house?

MR: When she and G were together, she moved out of her parents' house and went to work at the university, and they built a house that had parts in common. The front parts were separated, but the houses were connected at the back.

DM: What does that mean? You could enter into either house at the back? Two front doors and one back door?

MR: Yes. There was one backyard and in the front there were two living rooms, two bedrooms, and I think the common door gave access to the kitchen, the library, the backyard and two bathrooms.

DM: And did she inherit the whole house when G died?

MR: The matter is still pending with G's heirs.

DM: For the last seven years?

MR: Yes. There is a lawsuit going on in this respect.

DM: Who is suing who?

MR: She's been trying to have the heirs buy the house so she could build another one.

DM: It's like the comedian who tells of the gold watch that he got from his grandfather and he says, with tears in his eyes, 'He sold it me on his death-bed.' Right. Seven years ago? Right, okay. Of course I'm trying to understand how psychotic this girl is. The way she tells things and the absolute certainty with which she announces her theories. It certainly sounds pretty psychotic. 'All because of my origins: my father was German, my mother was Belgian, and my brother and sister married Brazilians, but I've stayed single.'

Well, it isn't true that she stayed single. It's true that in her one heterosexual relationship the fellow died, and she has had no others, but instead she's had three homosexual relationships. I mean, she has this very interesting capacity to explain everything. And it begins to look as if she lives in a world like you have said, of prey and predator: that is the kind of world she lives in, but there is a very delicately balanced situation between who is the prey and who is the predator, depending on who can play dead. She is so good at playing dead that one wonders how certain she is that these other people's deaths have been genuine and not just playing dead. She can't do anything with G's house, everything in there is sort of paralysed in the house which I presume is empty. Perhaps falling to pieces and so on. She can't go to Buenos Aires because G is buried there. Right, now you are courageously going on, to interpret the transference to her. Well, it isn't at all clear to me that she listens to anything you say.

MR: I try to keep alive.

DM: And yet she was furious at the beginning of this session, furious about something you said about intrauterine life and she threatened to abandon you and so on. Now it looks as if she has a conviction that there was a period in her life, in the womb, when everything was perfect: no pain, no hunger, no thirst … It looks as if she has threatened you because she fears that you have threatened this conviction she has about this happy period in the womb.

MR: Probably.

DM: Now, that seems to me to imply that she feels that you are on the verge of telling her something very different, which is that she was immobile in the womb – not happy, but immobile. And that even in the womb she was terrified and playing dead. Right, let's go on and see what happens in Phase Two.

MR: Phase Two: material A. This was the third session of the week and Elisa had been absent the day before. She enters my room looking very pale, despondent, and carrying in her handbag a book that she puts on a chair. As she lies down, she tells me that she's had severe stomach-aches with cramps and vomiting and that she had seen a gastroenterologist who had requested ultrasound exams to exclude a diagnosis of gallstones. She then says:

> 'Today I received an book from abroad that has an article on psychoanalysis; it is a super up-to-date encyclopaedia. I've been extremely anxious since Friday because tomorrow is the selection of professors for our department and I'm the chair of the board. I should not have accepted this position because I'm emotionally involved with the two nominees. H will be approved, but V won't; she is too childish and hasn't published anything in eight years. It's impossible to approve someone like this. If she doesn't pass, she will lose her job, and in the situation that the country is going through she won't be hired anywhere. Now I know, what I had yesterday was a fit because of this story. H's mother called my sickness a fit.'

I said I believed her sickness could be called pain and not 'a fit' or the like, or else she would not bring this fact to talk about here or be interested in reading psychoanalytical articles.

She arrogantly replies that she even intended to talk to Professor C, the elderly professor in the department, and hear his opinion about the case, but that she had not done that because she already knew what grades she would give to H and V.

DM: It isn't clear to me. Is this a university teacher's exam, for tenure? Now, does that mean that they have to sit an exam or simply that some efficiency report has to be made on them?

MR: Yes. At this point she was already the head of her department and was in charge of making a report. After some time, the teachers have to pass this test and she was the chair of the board. It is a test involving published works.

DM: Yes, but is there an examination? Do you mean nothing else counts but the weight of the papers that they have? Now, the question is: is that true or is that her way of understanding it?

MR: I believe it's true.

DM: In the military you have a commanding officer who writes your efficiency reports. It's simply one person that decides. So, there are two other people? But she is behaving not only as if it is entirely up to her, but also as if it's a matter of life and death.

MR: Yes. Hence the conflict.

DM: Right, okay. Yes, go ahead.

MR: She tells me a dream: *Last night I dreamt I was in a place that looked like paradise. There were flowers, rivers, lakes, and I was inside that world, fascinated by the exotic things around. I started to collect seashells from the floor and hold them in my hands, but they would turn into common stones and I would throw them away. Then I walked about and came to a crystal-clear lake where weird creatures swam. They were invertebrates, colorful octopuses, but when I came close to catch them, they had no life and were made of clear plastic. On the shore, there was a woman. She plunged into the water and came out holding a beautiful shell that opened and showed an exotic animal. I walk towards her and, as I come closer, I realise it was no animal, but a shapeless, lifeless form made of plastic.*

She continues: 'Now I remember another story, I don't even know if it can have any connection with this. This morning a colleague who came from another city to take a place on the examining board told me about the research he's been doing in his department about genetic manipulation. They produced a hen with a huge body mass, twice as big as a common hen. It is a mega-hen that grows in 60 days, with only one drawback: this super-hen has a high frequency of death by heart attack, as its heart is small and can't supply the huge muscle mass.'

DM: What a world she lives in! A world where everything that is beautiful turns lifeless and plastic and artificial the moment she touches it, and where science produces monsters that cannot survive. Now, this doesn't really look to me like simply the world of projective identification. At first this world of hers is described as nature's paradise: 'I was there, in that world, fascinated by the exotic things around. I started to collect seashells from the floor and hold them in my hands, but they would turn into common stones and I would throw them away.' Now, what did she say just before that … 'I've stayed single, but my brother and sister married Brazilians and this must have smoothed it over.' As if she had made some great sacrifice to spare them from being celibate, from being sterile, from being suicidal and so on. I think this goes beyond the ordinary grandiosity of projective identification. Well, let's go on.

MR: When she stopped talking, I felt petrified for a few moments, unable to think. Then I managed to say that she was bringing on that occasion her developed intellectual part with many functions – the chair of the board – along with her vulnerable emotional part that becomes sick and somatises. She brings an up-to-date book for me to learn how to take care of her; however, when I draw her attention to her fragile part, which she calls V, she escapes and leaves our relationship.

DM: Well, I think that's very good. She certainly has not petrified you, in fact.

MR: She wants to collect good, beautiful, alive, and colourful things with me, but she gets scared when she feels me so close by and tries to petrify me or turn me into a super-hen, which would have much to offer as food but would be of no use if it were dead.

DM: That really is an excellent interpretation. It really pulls it together. That you're this big hen with these double-sized mega breasts and so on … but you're not viable. It's quite right that she is going to condemn V as a part of herself, condemn her to death. Right, material B.

MR: She mumbles 'hum, hum' as a reply and remains silent until the end of the session.

DM: What did that 'hum, hum' sound like? I don't quite understand the music of 'hum, hum'. What does it mean?

MR: She would do this when she didn't want to listen to me.

DM: But do you the analyst ever make that sound, when you're listening – that's what I'm wondering?

MR: No.

DM: I do. My patients sometimes complain about my saying 'hum'.

MR: Material B. Monday session. Elisa says:

> 'This weekend I had to keep migrating from one corner of the house to the other: one side was too cold and the other had too much sunlight and got too hot. I eventually settled in a corner, where I could read something. I have this very dispersed way of studying; instead of stopping and getting deep into my reading, I restart it several times until I find myself far away from the topic I am reading about. I have to deliver a class on the physiology of vision and I drifted away to neurophysiology, trying to make correlations, and I got lost in themes that had nothing to do with the visual apparatus. I started reading, for example, about the influence of light in hormone secretion, etc.'

DM: Well, that's probably a beautiful description of what happens when she listens to you. But she could have said: 'Oh yes, I have a very dispersed way of listening to you. Instead of stopping and getting into your text, I begin to look into other things that I think are related to what you intend to say. Which carries me far, far away from anything you do in fact say.'

MR: I said that when she's with me, she wants me not to feel seduced by this whole universe surrounding human knowledge and to remain concentrated essentially on herself and her emotions. She seemed not to listen to me and said: 'While I studied the visual system, I thought of a few questions. A visual sign can be investigated in a sophisticated manner, one can study the code of one functioning neuron to record each signal, but nothing is known about decoding and realising how it all works, how the stimulus is resumed and processed in the mind. At this point, science stops and that's a mistake.' She makes a short pause and says she is teaching classes to replace V (whom she killed), the rejected co-worker, and therefore she has no obligation to know everything.

DM: Yes, she certainly is teaching you everything you need to know about things that you are particularly interested in. And she certainly didn't hear you or pay any attention to what you said. Of course, unfortunately, it sounds all very scientific, sophisticated, refined, the code of a neuron. And then it all stops, 'science stops, and that's a mistake.' Now, what does she mean? What is the mistake?

MR: I believe the mistake is in trying to understand her emotions.

DM: Yes, it certainly means coming up against the limits of your knowledge. Which is here called the brain. You can do all these clever and sophisticated things with the visual apparatus, but then suddenly you'll find yourself confronted with the brain and realise you don't know anything. I presume in the transference you are the brain, not just a mega-hen with these huge breasts, but a brain that knows how to think, that knows how to listen and observe. So something is happening that makes her realise that she is making a mistake in treating you in such a high-handed, insulting way, really. Then we hear that she is going to take over as substitute for V. That instead of killing her off, she finds herself actually identified and having to do V's job. And at that point she finds herself really pleading that she shouldn't be expected to know everything. As if her omniscience was simply compliance with the demands made upon her to know everything. Right. Now, you go to work on her again. Let's see what happens.

MR: I told her firmly that, if when I speak she runs away and cannot listen to me, it will not be easy for her to understand herself based on her internal signs. But I also said that she had an intuition that at the point where science fails or won't give her answers, maybe I could enter with the science of feelings, of human comprehension, and we could then speak in a language of emotions.

DM: Yes. I mean, that's very good. We don't have to speak the language of mathematics, to speak with some degree of precision. We can speak the language of emotions, which is a different kind of precision and worthy of the name of science.

MR: She says: 'This is not such an easy task as understanding neurophysiology. I feel that only now, after 20 years, I begin to study and understand, with the feeling that I'm actually learning the integrative processes of the nervous system. Over the past few years, much death, disease, and cancer happened in my life. I also had to work twice as hard in the department. Then I thought: 'Gosh, this sector never stabilises!' I have to teach classes that I've never taught before. In the end, these inheritances and losses mean more effort, more work for me; but, after all, I think I'm learning things I've never expected to learn.'

I felt that I had to decode Elisa's words firmly. In this session, she was patently emphasising her intellectual part that grows or develops when someone dies or is rejected.

DM: Yes. I mean, she really has listened to you this time. Because what she is saying is that her old theory, that survival was the only important thing, is perhaps not the ultimate value system really. That there's another value system, which you represent, called learning from experience and developing. Because here we are not dealing with a rigid, plastic, unchanging world. We're dealing with the world in constant flux, in constant change, and we're not trying to control it, we're trying to understand it a little bit. And it's not only that she's learning things she never suspected she would learn; she never suspected they existed to be learnt. So, you have had eight years of her teaching you how to be scientific. And she was certainly on the verge of killing you off. Whether you were an octopus, a shellfish or a mega-hen. Or a colleague named V. Or, as she threatened you at the beginning, if you dared talk to her like that she'd leave. She really threatened you, like the president of the board: 'If I had had to stay here after your interpretation at the end of the session, I wouldn't have tolerated it.' So, here's really a touch of humility in this high-handed, arrogant girl. It doesn't yet answer, for me, the question as to whether we're dealing with projective identification or something more psychotic. Right, Phase Three.

MR: Phase Three. Elisa communicates with me through dreams. In this session, she is more relaxed; she laughs as she speaks about her research on tonic immobility, tells me that she's been studying a family of newborn rats and that she found out that they only present immobility after birth and lose it as they grow up. Then she speaks about the film *Gorillas in the Mist*, saying that she identified with the American woman who had close contact with the animals. At this point, I make an interpretation: 'You expect to understand yourself better and not have to immobilise in this new phase of closer contact with me.'

She then says: 'I've been having dreams that reflect well this difficulty I have in going deeper into the analytic process.' She related a dream from the Friday night: *I dreamed I had to go up this steep slope to get here. I was carrying my nephew on my back, he was sick and he was heavy. The climb was hard and later I had to cross an entire forest. There were many ways to pass through it and I took one of them, the one that goes towards the hospital with glass walls; it was there that I wanted to go, that I had to go. When I got there, I entered the hospital and looked around; I saw the view outside the glass walls. I looked at everything and everything was beautiful: there was a stream and nature was so fascinating that I got distracted from the business of going to analysis. I felt I was going to be late.*

The same night she had another dream: *I had my nephew on my lap and he had to go to chemotherapy and I was the one in charge of applying it. There was this box of needles that I should use and all of them were bust or contaminated. It was an uncomfortable situation; I wanted to do something to relieve my uneasiness, and I couldn't.*

I felt the anguish in her speech, but she was quite close to me. I told her that, as a child, the little part within her comes to be treated. To do that, we must together break the glass walls that symbolise her difficulty in feeling her emotions, in connecting with me.

I notice that she feels moved and weeps until the end of the session, when I tell her that her emotional part had been taken by cancer, imprisoned like the part of the nephew that has malignant things inside him. She wanted to be a doctor, a mother by herself, alone, autochthonous, but she realised it was no longer possible to deal with herself on her own. Now she wanted to break down the glass wall to make it possible for me and herself to take care of her together.

DM: Oh, that's terribly good. So, it does look as if she is on the verge of emerging from projective identification and may not be psychotic. But I must say I'm not absolutely convinced about it. Very good! Hard work.

Participant: I would like to know what Dr Meltzer believes is more psychotic than projective identification?

DM: Well, of course, projective identification can be very primitive, and of course it can involve the person in all sorts of perversions and addictions and confusions and so on. But *living in* projective identification there is always a certain danger of falling into a delusional system and becoming unavailable to analytic contact, at least with a part of the personality. It doesn't always happen to the whole personality, but to the part of the personality that becomes schizophrenic, which then becomes unavailable to analytic therapy. It is my opinion, about this material, that this patient probably has been schizophrenic and the analyst has succeeded in making contact with non-schizophrenic parts of the personality which have lived in projective identification. That it should take eight years to accomplish that, and to be now on the verge of being able to do an analysis with it, seems to me not an unreasonable amount of time.

CHAPTER FOUR

A countertransference experience with an eleven-year-old-boy
(1996)

Alicia Beatriz Dorado de Lisondo

F elipe is an eleven-year-old boy who has a sister aged seven and another aged six months. The parents got married when the mother was seven months pregnant. Their marriage and family life is in a painful, fragile and stormy condition: the parents blame and accuse one other, especially about how to educate their child. The mother, depressed, insecure and frail, sees the father as someone obsessed with his attempts to assert his paternal function. He himself feels guilty, lacking in authority, undervalued, and responsible for the family misfortunes; in desperation he resorts to physical violence and shouting. Very talented in his own profession, he used to be alcoholic, and has now recovered from this thanks to his own psychoanalysis.

Both father and mother are undergoing psychoanalytic treatment. The paternal grandfather is a menacing shadow behind Felipe; he lived in an institution for the elderly and was considered emotionally deficient. The middle child is just the opposite of my patient: she is a very spoiled girl, a leader at school and apparently a model child who seems to teach her parents how to be parents. By contrast my patient found himself in the position of a black sheep.

At the time of my assessment of Felipe, he was very confused as his parents' marriage was going through a severe crisis, with continual quarrelling and the parents undermining one another's authority. Felipe had been a very difficult baby, the mother used to hold him on her lap for up to two hours to get him to sleep. She said that he did not properly sleep, he just drifted away. He was breastfed for thirteen months, despite the mother's severe postpartum depression. At four and a half years, he learned to read and write by himself and used to write his mother's name in his father's diary and next to it, the word 'help'. The father identified with the child's acute sensitivity and unhappiness, his resentment about the lack of emotional contact.

At age six, Felipe was referred to a neurologist owing to symptoms of astigmatism, hyperopia, and allergic rhinitis. He was diagnosed with neuropsychomotor instability associated with dyscrasia and anxiety attacks; the evolutionary neurological examination showed developmental retardation in areas involving attention and concentration and he was prescribed neuleptil.

At the age of seven, Felipe moved to a school where intellectual performance was highly rated. In his previous school he used to sit at the back of the classroom, where he was far from the teacher and tended to fight with his classmates. In the new school, it was very difficult for him to keep up with the academic level, and school exams were a torture. The parents decided to move him to another less demanding school. The session I am about to relate occurred at the time of this new change of school. Felipe did not adapt well socially to this school; he felt demeaned at attending a lower level institution; so the parents moved him back to the previous school, where at least he had friends.

Felipe accuses his parents of ruining his childhood and of beating him; he says his sister is better off because she had better parents.

Donald Meltzer: It is not unusual to have children who are retarded in all sorts of ways, when there is serious disagreement between the parents about the educational techniques, boundaries, and so on. The confusion that is engendered in the child by this early conflict between his parents seems, in this case, to go back to the fact that he was conceived outside marriage, unexpectedly. It is a source of conflict and blame. So it really goes back to his time in the womb.

It is interesting to hear him say that his sister is a better-developed personality because she has different parents. This is not just a random idea of the child's; it is an observation that his parents behave quite differently toward his sister. Not just toward the sister herself, but toward each other, in the atmosphere that the sister creates. Therefore, we really are dealing with a child who has a deep conviction of being troublesome, a troublemaker.

Alicia Lisondo: After my original assessment of Felipe I referred him to another colleague because I knew the emotional involvement that would be required and at that time I did not have sufficient availability. The parents stopped the treatment after four years, disappointed with its results. They had a trusting relationship with me and I was asked to interview Felipe again, and we started analysis three times a week.

The new issues were: megalomanic ideas, such as having to be very rich; repetitive obsessionality (the way he keeps his accounts and controls his money savings); he wants to build a city, to own a large home, and make trips to China, Rome, Japan, etc. Family life is difficult because he wants to control everything. If the family goes out for lunch on a Sunday, he does not want to go with them, but he demands his share of the expenses in cash. He suffers from great anxiety, which the parents illustrate by his biting his fingers and needing to urinate every fifteen minutes during the night, up to 30 times. He is incapable of coping with frustration; the parents give the example of his still printing his letters as he cannot produce a legible handwriting. His coordination is poor and he is not able to tie his own shoelaces. The parents interpret such difficulties as lack of perseverance or lack of manners. Felipe has emotional explosions when he is at risk of losing anything; he does not play sports, his socialisation is impaired, and intellectual computer games are his refuge. He envies his seven-year-old sister and fights a lot with her, but he loves his baby sister, and cares tenderly for her.

Both the parents and Felipe take the treatment seriously. I found Felipe a sad and tormented boy who expresses himself verbally in a moving way and inspires great pity and interest in me.

DM: Clarify something for me. He had a four-year psycho-analytic therapy? With different therapists, I guess. To whom did you refer him, a man or a woman? Which grade is he in at school?

AL: He is in the fifth grade.

DM: Is this fifth grade in keeping with his age or is he behind?

AL: He is at the appropriate grade for his age, but with the help of a huge team of private tutors.

I will now bring the first session of the week, a very special week because he has changed schools, and I was waiting for a family communication in order to organise the new schedule.

DM: How often is he seen?

AL: Three times a week: Tuesday, Thursday and Friday. This is a Tuesday session.

For the first time, he arrives with a colorful T-shirt with children's characters printed on it. He enters the room almost crawling, lies down on the couch and he always wants me to start by asking him something. If I ask, he can answer. After all, why does he always have to speak; he wants to be sure that I care for him. I interpret: 'So, to prove that I care for you, I am the one who has to stay here, in this place of so much despair.'

DM: I am not sure what you mean.

AL: What I mean is that I thought that he wanted me to be in the position of the one who has to speak, as this was a place of despair, so I can understand and care for him.

DM: You thought he wanted you to be in the same state of mind that he is in, because in his view, that would make it possible for you to understand him. Does he often lie on the couch?

AL: Yes, often, and generally he does not use his toy box.

DM: So, this probably has something to do with what he thinks goes on in his parents' analysis. It may boil down to his saying, 'I would like to be treated like a grown up.' This is how grown-ups behave: when you ask them something, they do not answer and they are eager to distribute feelings of despair. In fact, his idea about adult relationships is that they are constantly pushing despair into one another. However, how does that link with his wearing this colourful T-shirt, which I presume is something unusual. It is a fairly striking beginning for a session – the colourful T-shirt, dragging himself in, lying on the couch, and saying that he wants you to ask him questions so that he can not answer you and make you feel full of despair.

It seems to me to be in keeping with this whole idea about what it is to be an adult; and he is very ambitious to be an adult – he taught himself to write prematurely, and so on. His ideas about being an adult seem to include all of these obsessional preoccupations with money, with the desire to travel. And I would also think include going to the toilet 30 times a night. That is his idea of intimacy.

AL: He replies, 'I want you to tell me how can I make my father stop quarrelling with me. He has no patience, and most of all, he tells me that I am pretending, that I am faking it.' He persists with this demand, which turns into a kind of supplication. 'What are those quarrels about?' I ask him. He tells me they are the ones he told me about during the last session: about his difficulties at the new school, the long time he takes to do his homework, his fights with his sister, and so on. His father gets furious, threatens him, shouts and punishes him.

DM: The implication of this is that not only does he want to have a particular kind of intimacy with you, but he also feels that if you would instruct him how to behave, he could overcome all these difficulties. Simply by being obedient to you, he would not be slow, would not have any difficulties at the new school, would not fight with his sister, and would not make his father furious. He would be a good boy for you. In a way, he is saying, 'All I need is for the orders to be clear, and I would follow them.' In other words, he presents himself as a victim of the bad organisation of this family business. It is a kind of complaint against the bureaucracy.

AL: I interpret: 'You feel that you are the least important being in this world and you want to be helped to change.' He says, 'Yes, I do feel like that: I am the first child, I had my place. My sister came, occupied this place and what now? How can I get it back? Speak! Say something now! Speak!'

DM: You say he is the least important being and he agrees with you. He used to be the first person in line, until his sister came along.

AL: I try to create a space through silence; I am thinking about the new schedule that is being arranged. He insists, appeals, begs for an answer. I say, 'The question is the place that you have here with me; will it will be possible to find another time for your sessions or will you miss out?' He says 'Yes, I wanted you to see me at that other time I came. When I talk like this, am I behaving well? Am I doing the right thing, am I cooperating with the analysis? Is this the right way to do it?'

DM: He is insisting on clarification of the analysis' administration, which means really that you should assume a dictatorial relationship to his parents and family and put everything in order, which means to put him back in the first place as the eldest child. It is what we might call a very political attitude. That is, what we need is really a strong leadership, a military government.

AL: I tell him, 'You wonder if I consider you able to collaborate, to relate, since you feel you are very bad and so you are left out.' He replies, 'I am afraid of being always wrong, will I be like my grandfather?' He sits and holds his head in both hands; while sitting on the couch he bends in a way that breaks my heart, inspires deep compassion in me.

'Sometimes, I want to kill myself. Ah! I changed school, is that a good thing, to have changed school? What do you think – will it solve anything? In this new school, in the fifth grade, there are three classes; I went to the one where I have friends.'

I say, 'You wonder if a change is possible here, in your analysis, a change far beyond the timetable change. Can I see that you are able to make friends? Will I make an effort to give you a space here?'

He says, 'I am a teenager, not thirteen but I am eleven and I want to go to another room – [he points to the adult room] that room – that room is more comfortable than this one!' He speaks insistently. I say, 'I think you would like to make the time run faster to escape from this painful life, but you want to be recognised as someone who is eleven years old.' He speaks about

Bugs Bunny and the Tasmanian devil, and I say: 'I see a young man, eleven years old, but we also need give space to this boy who feels he is a devil. To change this situation we need to work to achieve change inside yourself.'

For the first time, he throws a velvet cushion at me and I catch it as if we were starting a ball game. This lasts a few minutes, then he shakes the cushion in front of me, very close to my face. I blink and say, 'Are you testing me, so see what I am like inside? Can I stand being shaken?' He says, 'Do you care for me, or do you only care about the money my father pays you? Answer me, because that is my question: do you love me or is this only a professional job, it is just an appointment? Tell me, answer me, please!'

I say, 'You want to know if I am attached to you for what you really are.' He turns around quickly to look at me, to surprise me, and he really does surprise me when he says 'You're not looking at me.' At that moment I was reminded of my mother's osteoporosis and I find myself thinking about structural deterioration. Why did this come to mind at that moment?

I say, 'You want to know if I am reliable, if I am here for real, if you can inspire a good relationship.' He says, 'You know I changed school, I must be on time. How can we arrange things here?' He looks at the watch; it is time to stop. He asks, 'Is it time to go away? Let me be here a bit longer, I don't want to go away, let me stay, just one minute longer.' I say, 'You want to stay longer in order to feel accepted; when our hour finishes it is the same as being outside. I will change our times to be sure our work together can continue, and I will phone you.'

I follow him to the waiting room and I turn on the light because it is getting dark. He insists again that our timetable must change and he wants to know the new schedule.

After that session, in the evening, his mother phones me and says that her son had forgotten to give me a letter where she explained the change of school, and the need to change his session times.

In the next session, with the new schedule in place, he tells me in detail about the movie *The Last Emperor.*

DM: Let us stop a minute and talk before we go on to the next session. I am trying to understand what sort of world this boy inhabits and what sort of concepts of the world he has, because quite clearly he is in great distress and very urgently desires to be in harmony with you. Now, it seems to me that his ideas of being in harmony with you are, as I said, very bureaucratic, very military, very based on ranking, prestige and other social values.

His idea is that he is an eleven-year-old adolescent, and he says that as if it were a rank in the army: when you become an adolescent, one of that rank, you have certain privileges, and certain responsibilities or requirements, all perfectly clear. Now, that in a sense is very characteristic of the latency period child, to interpret the world in those hierarchical terms. But it is the meaning of these different hierarchic levels which he wants to be clear about, as when he says, 'Do you care about me, love me, or is just the money my father pays you that you care about?' You can see from this that his need to be cared about and loved is firmly established, but what isn't established is any idea of how it comes about. He has only a concept of progressing up to the next rank in the ladder. There is no concept of development but only one of social progress. He has no concept of intimacy which would allow for a concept of development.

We seem to be at a moment when his social confusion is at the maximum because of this change of school, change of schedule, etc. He is very sensitive to the question of whether he is being promoted or demoted. He clearly has a sort of catastrophic concept of demotion: that you go down the ladder and eventually you will be thrown in the rubbish.

Now, there is established in his mind another representation, that contains a developmental promise, and that is your attention to him. Your attention and interest in him is not the same as saying, do you care for him or do you love him. 'Are you looking at me?' is the way he expresses himself. He would like to have eyes in the back of his head so that he can observe whether you are looking at him, when he is turned away from you. But lacking eyes in the back of his head, he has to play this trick on you – turning away and suddenly turning back to see if you are looking at him.

Of course, we cannot possibly know why you had your mother's osteoporosis in mind at that moment, but I think what it means is that you felt his eyes are really X-ray eyes, looking inside you to detect structural defects in your interest in him: that you felt, at that moment, that he was trying to evaluate whether your interest in him was like a good firm bone, or whether it was something that looks correct from the outside, but inside is rather weak and fragile, and could easily be broken or distracted.

I think the response in your mind showed an understanding that what he needs is an interest that is very firm and strong; and he is figuring out whether you have that quality of character. It is a quality of interest, that sort of interest which can be deployed to him but can be deployed to other children as well. You are able to pay attention to him because you are an attention-paying person. And that is quite different from caring for him or loving him; it is something much more related to the meaning of psychoanalysis. Can you take an interest in him, and that means, really, can you see his potentialities.

Now this of course is the real parental position. That at whatever age and in spite of little sisters like this who seems so perfect, children are not in their characters and in their behaviour admirable and lovable, except for the fact that one's imagination can see what sort of adults they are going to develop into. It is a function of imagination. Parents do not love babies, they are tremendously interested in babies because they can imagine them growing up and developing. This is the reason that other people's children look lovable. Your own children seem lovable because you have the day-to-day, minute-to-minute intimate knowledge of them that enables you to imagine their developmental process.

Now, this boy brings up the matter of testing your firmness when he begs to stay a minute longer. I do not think it is in fact correct at this point that he wants to stay longer in order to feel accepted. The reason he begs you to let him stay longer is to test your firmness, to test for the lack of osteoporosis in your character. When you tell him 'Our time is up' this does not mean he will then be out of your mind; for when he leaves the room at the end of session, he does not leave your mind; he has a place in your mind that is not in any danger of being taken away by a little sister. And changing the schedule to guarantee your work together is certainly reassuring to him, as is your promise to phone him; but he has, you find later, forgotten or refused to give you the letter from his mother, which has the information about changing the schedule.

AL: I think he forgot, because the letter was with him all the time, in the session. I could not give him the new schedule unless I knew the school timetable.

DM: I am more inclined to believe that he resents you having any contact with his parents at all, because that arouses his anxiety that you are a hired servant, concerned with the money. That is why I do not think that at this point the problem is really the schedule. I think the problem is about whether he is in your mind between the sessions. Let us go on to hear about *The Last Emperor*.

AL: I have another session, but I would like perhaps to reflect with you on some other issues. When there is a primary deficit, as there seems to be in Felipe's case, what would be the changes in technique brought by another theoretical approach? I think, for example, of the work of Anne Alvarez or of Jean Bégoin.

DM: I am not really a fan of dissecting and analysing theories. It is very important to have your technique and to stick to it, and not to vary. I know it brings me in some conflict with Anne and Bégoin, but by no means is it a criticism of their methods of working, which are very much in the spirit of the way Mrs Tustin worked. I am in favour of developing a technique that is very firm and very consistent and that has its origins in your imaginative relationship to the patient as a developing organism. I do not agree with the theories that argue that it is necessary to adapt the techniques of adult analysis to the special needs of children.

This has of course been an issue since the very beginnings of child analysis. Mrs Klein's attitude was that Anna Freud and her school were employing a seductive technique. And that it was pretty ineffective at penetrating into the unconscious of the child. Now, I am inclined to agree with that attitude: that the purpose of the analytic technique is not to cure the child but to penetrate with an understanding of the unconscious. Here the questions of positive and negative transference are of very little therapeutic importance; since to behave in a way that is intended to strengthen the positive transference is not in the interest of children who have a great need to express an experience of negative transference. I think that it is better to accept what comes along in the transference, to accept the countertransference response in yourself, and to rely on your imaginative relationship to the patient as a developing organism.

This means a very fundamental change, away from interest in curing psychopathology toward interest in development. In my experience, if you pay attention to the evolution of the transference, then in fact the psychopathology gets resolved in the course of the patient's development. Now, I may not be doing justice either to Anne or to Jean Bégoin, but I have had enough personal experience working together with them in seminars and so on, to have a fair idea that we do not agree about these matters.

What is the second reflection?

AL: Also, another matter arose from Jean Bégoin's work. This seems to me to emphasise mental pain, and the right to the construction of subjectivity, and a different approach to destructiveness. I would like to talk about these new advances in very disturbed patients, from within the Kleinian metapsychology. How to approach destructiveness?

DM: Certainly there are people who emphasise a great deal the problem of mental pain. Mental pain is of course a very important function in the mind and in development; but the problem in mental pain is not the painfulness of the pain, the problem is about the attitude toward the pain. And it is my opinion that as an analyst you do the patient very little service when you join him in taking an interest in the painfulness of his pain, instead of helping him to taking an interest in the *meaning* of his pain. That seems to me to be a very fundamental distinction.

Of course it sounds hardhearted to say that you are not concerned with the painfulness of the pain, but it seems to be a very clear clinical fact. The more you can take an interest in the meaning of your pain, the greater tolerance of pain you can acquire.

It seems to me a fact that psychoanalysis does not much diminish the painfulness of life processes. We certainly can diminish the confusion, but I think we have little or no capacity to diminish the fundamental pains of living. Now, this has been a failure of psychoanalytic conceptualisation from the very beginning of Freud's preoccupation with pleasure and pain. And it is really only with Bion's work that we are in a position to think and talk about the meaning of the pain, rather than its painfulness. And, this of course is really in many ways the essence of what has come to be called the post-Kleinian position: that we as analysts are in pursue of the meaning of things, and we are not medical men seeking to prolong life, to diminish pain, to rescue and so on.

AL: The third issue concerns parents in child psychoanalysis, in times of impasse. I had met with Felipe's parents in the previous week, at the father's request, and to understand what was going on. Why a change after only two months of class? And my question was not the school; the question was an attempt to investigate the impasse. A change of school was not only a problem of Felipe's.

DM: I am pretty convinced that you will make very little headway by trying to manage the family situation. When this boy says that he and his sister have different parents he is making an astute observation. What he means is not only that their parents behave differently with them but also that they have a different transference to their parents. It is my opinion that children's relationship to their parents is just as much transference as is their relationship to the analyst. And their parents respond with countertransference just as analysts do.

The trouble is that parents are much more likely to act in the countertransference than to think in the countertransference. What happens quite regularly in child analysis is that as the transference to the analyst develops, the pressure on the parents as transference objects diminishes and the pressure on them to act in the countertransference diminishes. Therefore, after about six months the behaviour of the child in the analytic situation and their behaviour at home are as different as you could possibly believe. And the drawback of this is that the parents tend to think that the child has been cured and are eager for the expenses of the treatment to be brought to a close.

Participant: This is a question that has to do with the imaginative capacity of the analyst. It is known that Melanie Klein had an extraordinary clinical imagination. I would like to listen to you about this because you also made many references to the patient's imaginative capacity.

DM: Yes, I mean it is true that patients like analysts have very variable imaginative capacities. Now, the differentiation is not really so much a quantitative one because many patients, and many analysts too, have a very flexible imagination that can move very rapidly, change, and shift about very quickly. You can see this in an exaggerated form in the way some children may very quickly cover a page with little drawings that are full of imaginative objects, but you can see by examining them that in fact they are all simply variations, permutations and combinations of simple sadistic themes.

The important thing is the question of richness of imagination, which as I mentioned before hinges on the differentiation between received symbols and autonomous symbol-formation. Our children these days are bombarded with received symbols and, of course, many of them can produce this very flexible and rapid turnover of received symbols in their speech, their drawings, their play, and so on.

Now the thing that is difficult to see in Bion's theory of thinking is this differentiation between the alpha function that produces autonomous symbols and the alpha function that uses received symbols. The essential difference is between alpha function performed by the internal object, and alpha function performed by the self.

For instance, the art world today is really tormented by this quest for originality. And the originality of course turns out not to be original at all. Just like children's drawings, it turns out to be simply permutations and combinations, as you can see very clearly for instance in the work of the surrealists. The famous dripping clock of Dali is not an autonomous symbol; it is a paradoxical variation on the clock as a symbol for time.

Now, with a child like this, the therapist's capacity for autonomous symbol-formation, it seems to me, is very great, because routine interpretation is not going to touch such a child. I think that with this kind of child you have to be able to think in terms of: 'what sort of world is he living in?' And that places a great stress on your capacity for creative imagination.

It does not seem to me that he is at all like either an autistic child or a psychotic child. I have described him as a child who is living in a bureaucratic world, a rather military government in his mind. He seeks to make the emotional and passionate in his nature obedient to rigid and clear directives. And his demand on the therapist to be that kind of strong leader is not compatible with a psychoanalytic inquiry. That problem comes up most clearly in this particular session at the moment when he turns away and turns back quickly and he says, 'You are not looking at me?'

This arouses in the therapist, as she has confided to us, this extraordinary bit of countertransference. The challenge made to her capacity for creative imagination requires that she utilise her countertransference to understand the meaning of the transference. And creative imaginative psychoanalytic work depends very heavily on noticing these countertransference phenomena.

CHAPTER FIVE

The birth of a baby and premonitions of the depressive position
(1996)

Alfredo Colucci

The diagnosis of this patient, whom I will call Roberto, was clinical narcissism. He is almost 40 years old, has been in analysis for a year and a half, and has four sessions a week with me. I will not hand out copies of this material even though the patient has given me his permission to present it here.

Donald Meltzer: Just out of curiosity, if the patient had not given you his permission, what would you have done?

Alfredo Colucci: I would have talked about another patient.

DM: I am interested in this question regarding confidentiality. Would you ask his permission to submit this material to an ordinary supervision?

AC: No.

DM: Would you ask the patient's permission to talk to your wife about this case?

AC: No, I would not either.

Participant: His wife is an analyst.

DM: I was not talking about the colleague; I was talking about the wife. This issue of confidentiality is so complex that it becomes a little hypocritical.

AC: Throughout the first year of analysis, the patient brought dreams which took up more and more space in the sessions. Their function seemed to be to create a kind of dream-blanket which made emotional contact with me difficult. The theme of loss is frequent in his material.

I will present two sessions: one from a Friday and the other from the Tuesday following. The session on Friday (at 7 pm) was the last session of the week and the usual Saturday session was cancelled due to a trip that I made.

At this stage the patient was very satisfied with his professional life and with the atmosphere of harmony at home (his wife had accepted the baby's name, which had been talked about during the analysis). At a certain point in the session he says: 'I am living through the pregnancy and the beginning of a new activity. It is an important part of my identity. What I learn here becomes possible out there. I couldn't do it on my own.'

DM: Let's talk about this. It is a kind of honeymoon presided over by this foetus which has not yet been born. It is interesting to see how this baby makes itself present. This is one of the mysteries about the power of a child. When a newborn is brought to any situation in which there is a group of people, they can hardly look at anything except the baby. Often they cannot even talk about anything else.

I do not intend to explain why this is so, but in analysis we see many indications that this is exactly what the baby feels in this situation: that all eyes are on him or her. Patient and analyst tend to take the credit for the impact of the baby's existence, which I think it is okay in a sense, provided we bear in mind that the credit belongs to something which is not quite theirs. That is, they are somehow celebrating an event of nature, and while psychoanalysis is not an event of nature, it becomes a part of the family life. Patient and analyst find themselves celebrating something similar to a honeymoon but closer to a religious service.

Participant: At the beginning of this session, it was mentioned that the analyst was going on a trip instead of the Saturday session. Wouldn't there be here some hostility to the analyst? At first, it seemed to me the session was not a honeymoon.

DM: It is really surprising that, despite these facts you have mentioned, there is an atmosphere of cooperation. We might expect the room to be filled with ambivalence. What does he mean by 'the new activity'?

AC: The patient wishes to get closer to the analyst.

DM: We do not know that. The report does not mention what he thinks it means to be an analyst. Most patients, in a positive transference atmosphere, want to be the analyst, but I think this should be heard the same way we hear children say they want to be like mummy or daddy. This is normal projective identification: they already are analysts; they are analysing the children, the wife, the friends, and have a large number of patients. Normally, this phase is followed by another, in which the last thing they want in the world is to be analysts. When they realise they are not ideal patients, but difficult ones, they think to themselves that being an analyst means having a practice full of patients like them, so the effort is not worth it.

In my opinion, it is a shame that people can apply and be accepted for training before they complete the analysis itself because, many times, the disappointment comes during the training, during the course. It would be better if this disappointment came before, like the natural disappointment of a child over idealisation of its parents, rather than during the training. Because the purpose of idealisation is to lead to disillusion. Comprehension, which can be a consequence of disillusion, consists of the fundamental difference between self and object, that is, the difference between identification with the parents as external objects, and the identification with internal objects. This is what forms a person's character.

But let's go back to our man to see what is going on with him.

AC: Tuesday session. The first session of the week. I begin after a six-minute delay. He comes in, smiles as usual, quickly lies down on the couch, and says: 'My wife seems to feel the time is nearly here. I don't know if it is because of the uterus; it seems she is more contracted. That is how I understand what she says.'

DM: The honeymoon is over. We cannot put the blame entirely on the six-minute delay; however, we need to ask about the countertransference too. But this can be left for the analyst.

The expression 'it seems' is important because it is an acknowledgement that you cannot observe the meaning of things directly: we can only grasp it by thinking about the observations. So, the meaning of things comes down to 'it seems' and this is a disillusion. Go on.

AC: He continues: 'She has rested more, has complained of a bit of pain and has kept to herself more, has been quieter.'

DM: She has kept to herself more: this is the great disillusion. The emotional contact between people leads to an isolation, as if each person withdrew into himself or herself, regarding the other. He tries to explain it in terms of what is happening within the wife's uterus: 'It seems she is more contracted.' Is he talking about the uterus inside her or about her vagina? Is he talking about the way she talks or about her mouth? Because the disillusion of the interrupted emotional contact tends to bring back all the confusion about lack of confidence and about contact zones. He is talking about the solitude of individuality. This is the essence of disillusion, and what is called solipsism in philosophy. This is the fundamental isolation of each person in relation to others. The only possible comfort is the kind of contact you can have with internal objects, which I thought they were celebrating in that religious service of the previous session.

AC: I ask him what he felt when he saw his wife in pain, walking from one side to the other, and keeping to herself more. He laughs and says: 'Now I am thinking, I wonder if the delivery time has come.' At this moment, he makes sudden movements to hold himself onto the edge of the couch, trembles and holds firmly onto the edges.

DM: This is very interesting; he suddenly identifies himself with a baby about to be pushed and expelled outside, into the world.

AC: The patient says: 'I tell her that it is the nature of the adaptation, that this is how it works. The obstetrician said she would feel contractions, but this also affects the emotions. I have a feeling that delivery will be soon, that the time of the delivery has come.' I say he has been waiting for me from Friday to today, four days; he wants the delivery to be soon.

DM: It is very good how the analyst makes this connection between the analytical situation and the patient's experience with his wife, and through her, with the baby. And also how the problems he calls adaptation are clearly, at this point, problems caused by letting go of the idealisation – which is what the baby has to face at the moment it is born, pushed to the outside world and having to make the fundamental adaptation that is breathing.

AC: The patient says: 'The rhythm of the weekend affected me, as we did not have a session on Saturday. The beginning of today's session ... wait a minute ... I was anxious' (there is a silence). I point out the unknown and the waiting.

DM: Yes, birth is not so gradual; the pregnancy and the foetus' development might be, but birth is cataclysmic. 'Hold onto the couch!' It is very concrete the way he holds onto the couch.

AC: I say: 'Yes, and you are afraid I cannot stand your anxiety.' He says: 'Now I am a little confused, because it is either one or the other: either I feel anxious here or I feel anxious with my wife. Where should I feel anxious?' I notice the tense atmosphere of the session is gone. The patient says: 'I am trying to see why I am troubled. What comes to mind is that the pregnancy is gradual and uncertain; it depends on the baby and on my wife. I am taking part in a process that has two other people who do not depend on me, that is, only as a father and a husband.'

DM: What a deception!

AC: He says, surprised: 'It could be the beginning.'

DM: The analyst said before, 'You are afraid I may not be a good container for your anxiety.' Be a good container for a patient's anxiety and live it as if it were his. So, if the patient is holding onto the couch, feeling as anxious as if he were the baby who is about to be born, the analyst becomes the mother who is worried about the possibility that the baby may not be born alive, that it may not have all its fingers and so on.

AC: I say 'You are surprised. It is the desire that the final phase may end soon. Today, we are starting the first session of the week. You want to end the analysis, the work, the pregnancy ... is there an end to these things?' The patient says: 'Beginning, middle and end, it seems. Pregnancy ends, life starts out there, outside the womb.' The session time is over.

DM: This is a reference to another great disillusion, obscured by this gradual process in which one session follows the other, and a week is followed by another week, and time seems circular. Sometimes, it is a beneficial circle, sometimes it is a vicious circle, but it is always circular. With the urgency of this uterine condition, time suddenly stretches and becomes linear and the horizon appears to be what Mrs Bick calls a dead end. This means each session has its end, and each goodbye may be the last one. A fact of life. It is a beautiful aspect of analysis, but it has some superficiality, like everything related to pregnancy, either the patient's or his wife's pregnancy.

As I said, when a baby comes into a room, everything and all eyes converge on it. So, in a sense, when the pregnancy is in the analytical setting, everything is focused on it. And under this perspective not only is there anxiety, especially when there have been previous losses, but the situation is also infiltrated by a kind of optimism. This is part of the fact that the construction of a baby is such a mysterious process that it is absolutely beyond the control of the self. So, he is a little disappointed at being just the father, but he will also be disappointed to be just the mother, as it is a process that is not anybody's construction. Together with the optimism and the artificial hope, counterbalanced by the anxiety regarding the life and safety of the baby, he also realises this linearisation of time and the dead end.

This is an essential part of accepting reality, that was denied by the atmosphere of the first session (as I believe religious beliefs are also a way of denial). It would be very useful for development if people *hoped* for the existence of a heaven, of another life and so on, but it is easier for people to *believe* in heaven. They prefer to deal with it as if it were a belief and not a hope. Christians do not say: 'I hope that my Redeemer lives'; they pray: 'I know that my Redeemer lives.' The same happens in the analytic setting when the realisation of the difference between internal and external objects emerges as a belief and takes on similar traces to religious fanaticism. What could counterbalance it would be what Bion, inspired by Keats, called 'negative capability' – the capacity to remain in uncertainty, without trying to anticipate fact and reason. In material such as this, it is apparent how the optimism of beliefs is welcomed as they seem to reach beyond the consulting room to patients' marriages, their work-places, all worldly relationships. It is a type of euphoria and it is extremely welcome.

But here comes the moment of disillusion in which this delicate balance between the realisation of reality – linear time, the dead end – and the adoption of cynicism or pessimism takes shape. It is an important moment in any analysis, but here it is being pushed by the baby who presides over this situation. I emphasise the fact that the analytical process is being pushed artificially because after the baby is born, all these processes will reappear and they will have to be dealt with all over again.

The analyst acknowledges this and says: 'You seem surprised; you wish this final stage would end soon. Today we are starting the first session of the week and you want to end the analysis, the work, the pregnancy.' This is the acknowledgement that the patient wants to end the analysis at this point. As players say: 'Quit the game while you are winning.' I think the analyst was correct to point out that the patient wanted to end the analysis at that moment. And the patient said: 'What else is left for us to do? I am happy.'

Discussion

Participant: I would like to ask a question which may not seem exactly what is being focused upon here today, but it has to do with the theoretical issue mentioned previously. The question comes from the impression I have about this patient. He gives me the impression of being a frightened person. I imagined a young latency child who goes on his own to school by bus for the first time, still in a transitional situation, when the mother says: 'You can go, there is no danger, and nothing is going to happen.' This is a model; it came to my mind because there are losses mentioned in the history, that is, violent experiences, as if the boy were robbed on the corner after leaving home.

The question previously raised here was about 'history'. It was suggested the analyst should in a way put the pieces of information the patient gives about his life between parentheses or forget them. Now, the losses may sound like a 'trauma' to the analyst and the analyst has a frightened child in front of him. I wanted to know if Dr Meltzer works with the notion of trauma in this historic sense.

DM: If we take abortion as a model, the issue, in linguistic terms, is in the difference between abortion and miscarriage, a difference which in Portuguese is made by the modifiers 'spontaneous' *versus* 'induced' abortion. Either way, the origin of this failure, this defeat of life, is always uncertain. Therefore, it is not surprising that the parents feel depressed and guilty when there is a 'spontaneous' abortion as they cannot be sure they did not contribute to it. This is one of the reasons why I would not see these abortions as traumas.

In fact, I do not find any space in analysis for the concept of trauma, as I think this concept reinforces a type of persecutory anguish that prevents confronting the problem of uncertainty and the issue of responsibility. This includes even our attitude as to what influence the environment exerts over the child: that is, if it has a real impact or only a relative influence on the child, just reinforcing the rudimentary influences and in a way the primitive ones; each moment involves judgement and decision.

So, even when we talk about temperament, I think we may be avoiding the issue of the baby's capacity to judge and decide. It is true that babies seem to differ from one another in terms of temperament from birth. On the other hand, foetal ultrasound studies make inevitable the suspicion that there is already mental life in the uterus, that what is in there is not only solely a baby with its umbilical cord and its placenta: there is also the contact and the communication with the outside world and with the mother's mind through her voice, attitudes and thoughts. And through all that the mother's mentality, and through her, the father's mentality are printed on the baby.

These considerations are important in the issue of medical abortion. The idea may be unbearable that what is done is no less than killing a person. Even resources such as intrauterine devices may be considered as the introduction of a small abortive influence inside a woman's uterus. Life is complicated.

In short, I think the material is very beautiful that shows this crucial moment in any analysis, the moment which is the threshold of the depressive position. But in this case we saw something being pushed forward in time, something that will have to be recovered and reworked with more peace and quiet.

Still, if in an incident like this, the metapsychology of what happens could be clearly established, it could be later used as a guide to help when the process becomes difficult and the threshold of the depressive position has to be faced. As if we, as people, said to the patient: 'We know what is going to happen. As we saw when your wife was pregnant and at a certain point you held onto the couch, and at another moment, you felt euphoric and believed the analysis had come to an end. As if it were a condensation of the type of experience you are trying to face now.'

It is indeed very beautiful material.

CHAPTER SIX

Overcoming a preformed transference
(1996)

Paulo Cesar Sandler

G iulio, aged 40, came to analysis a year and ten
months ago, having four sessions a week. He is the
last of six siblings (the eldest male, with four sisters
in between), and father of three sons and a daughter born
during six years of marriage. A Brazilian national who also
enjoys a foreign citizenship, Giulio had privileged educational opportunities both in Brazil and abroad, and has risen
to the top of his engineering profession.

As soon as we begin our first consultation, he spontaneously starts to tell me about his family of origin, mainly about
his deceased father, who trained in business administration in
Sweden at a time when this was rare in Brazil. He came from a
landowning class going back to the colonial era and where large
families were a mark of status. A wellknown and well-respected
man in the Brazilian elite, he is described by Giulio as an
emotionally distant person, a 'typical South American macho',
prone to adopt authoritarian rules and to boasting about his
relations with influential people. When his sons reached adulthood he lived with a former secretary – 'a beauty' – until the
end of his rather long life. One of the father's many demands

was that his sons had to be outstanding sportsmen, preferably Olympic standard; but none of them could fulfil this ambition for him.

I prefer to leave patients to report spontaneously rather than asking questions; and it was only about five months later that I learned Giulio's mother is still alive, at least physically. She is of Swedish nationality; Giulio says she had misgivings about Brazilian educational methods and insisted her sons should have a Swedish education. She refused to follow her husband's wish to have ten or twelve children – 'she complained even about six pregnancies' (he laughs, as if telling a joke). She could not understand his cultural habits yet never openly quarrelled with him. Although the father had studied in Sweden, he refused to pay for his sons to study abroad, yet the mother managed to arrange it by means of courting wealthy industrialists and marrying off her daughters. According to Giulio his mother was unable to be sincere, 'always disguising her real intentions and purposes'. His tone is that of a dry, non-committal report, giving me the impression that his mother was unable to have meaningful emotional contact with him and that she presented matters to him as a *fait accompli*.

Giulio did not express any open resentment against his parents; for the first six months of the analysis he would just smile or laugh during his reports or make an occasional comment such as 'isn't this weird'. He reminded me of a TV series from the fifties called *Father Knows Best* in which the pet dog laughed at the end of each show, aping the actors. Following the source of my own free association, I believe the actor in the series was a heavy drinker and had at one point attempted suicide.

At our first meeting Giulio told me he had left his previous job 'in search of new experiences'. He talked about his dual nationality and whether he should keep his Swedish citizenship which would mean he paid more taxes (he laughs); then he says his own wife was born in Sweden, and they agreed to give their children international names. He has a British-sounding accent himself, and his pronunciation is not Portuguese; sometimes he has difficulty finding a word in Portuguese, and I ask him to talk in English if he prefers – something that he does occasionally, switching between languages. My emotional experience, listening to his explanations mixed with justifications (after all, I had not asked him anything) was that I was witnessing a self-reassuring verbalisation. It seemed to me that he was talking with someone whose ideas corresponded with his own, but this 'someone' was not I.

After one year and half in his new job, he felt he was encountering serious difficulties in adapting to the Jewish milieu of the organisation, a 'city of London place'. He says he understands Jews for he had a Jewish friend in high school whose family environment was 'the opposite' of his, being warm and conversational, 'emotional and sensitive'; but this friend's parents disapproved of *goyim*, even though they all 'loved analysis' and had psychoanalytic treatments. As time went on, from further descriptions of this friend, I learned more about Giulio's personal meanings given to qualifications such as 'emotional and sensitive': words which seemed to imply a person and a family with no capacity for containment or self-restraint. There was a splitting off of hate and of anti-semitic feelings. There were definite but indirect indications of resistances to his own religious heritage (his father Catholic, his mother Lutheran), but not as contemptuous as his attitude towards the Jews. His Jewish friend (whose name he never uttered) was 'a brilliant guy, very intelligent as all Jews are, but too complicated – he complicates the life of anyone near him.' He never explained what kind of complication, even when I asked. He would immediately jump to descriptions of his new work in Stockholm: 'Now I am obliged to work with those yuppies who come from all over the world, social climbers who want to be rich and spare no tricks in getting what they want. They conduct business in a very aggressive way. My boss is a typical Jew. Well this is their way, they do not this because they are bad, and they are educated like this. It is cultural, they scream all the time, call names, and cannot respect any social rules of discretion.'

He told me he had never dreamed in his whole life; but his Jewish friend would recall his dreams. 'Well, he was homosexual, you know. Dreams belong to women: they love telling people their dreams. Men do things; women just dream and do nothing. They dream of finding a magic prince who will marry them, you know.'

After almost one year working in the 'stressful condition' of his new job, he had for the first time consulted a psychiatrist, who made the fashionable diagnosis of a 'panic syndrome', which was eagerly taken by Giulio as a justification to enter into an unthinking mode: 'See? I am not crazy, this is an organic condition!' In his opinion the Swedish psychiatrist was a trustworthy authority; whereas it seemed to me that he had no qualms about making false reassurances about how Giulio's condition was 'normal', environment-induced, and could be resolved by medication. He gave him a new serotonin reuptake inhibitor, which was taken with a quasi-religious adoration: 'Much better than Prozac!' I ask him if he had any experience with Prozac, to which he replied, no.

At the same time, he entertained, probably unconsciously, serious doubts about his way of living. But he seemed not to hear what he was saying; I cannot say that he was telling me those things directly, personally. It seemed more an automatic form of throwing things out, irrespective of the person who was with him. His talk was a continual complaint but he did not seem to hear his own complaints. This pattern was repeated in the ensuing sessions. Some of his doubts about his life centred on his not pursuing an artistic career. Then they switched to the fact that he did not have a high post in the federal government. He usually began his phrases with a rather affirmative, but questioning, 'See ...' or 'You know ...': 'See, industries and business are just numbers. This is their only interest. But I take pleasure in the arts and literature. You know, I took a music course at the university, and when I finished it – got to all classes, did not miss any – my teacher told me that I mastered the techniques, but she did not feel my interpretations had any personal subjective quality.' I took this comment as a sign of a remote, but seeable – at least to me, under the analytical vertex – contact with himself; but the comment was made as if by another person (the music teacher) and as if about a person other than himself.

Progress of the analysis

Giulio soon developed a quasi-automatic way of conducting analysis. He would come for one, two or three weeks and then miss the sessions of the following one or two weeks, then re-initiate the cycle. His absence is always accompanied by a justification: 'I had to travel, I was sick', etc. The same quasi-automatism is present in his actions. I will fetch him from the waiting room where he is usually seated in a chair, immovable. As soon as he sees me, as if he did not sense my presence in advance, he rises up, bows under a smiling compliment, says a commonplace phrase about the weather, or about politics, and hesitates on entering the consulting room. 'Please, you first', as if he were a gentlemanly master of ceremonies at a party, which in my view constitutes an attempt to disguise the reality of his bossy posture. He displays a covert hesitation in lying down, feigning that he likes it when in fact he dislikes it. Sometimes he quotes his height as a hindrance to lying down – he is six and half feet, an achievement he finds admirable, as if it were his own doing. Usually he leaves his feet hanging off the couch, even though he could settle more comfortably.

Often he asks me if I know such-and-such a person – usually wellknown and wealthy personalities – or if I have read this or that book, or seen this or that film or art exhibition. He ends his queries telling me that he has known them since their infancy, or read the book years ago, or saw the art exhibition last week. He seems to believe in stereotypes: what a woman is ('women dream, men act'), what a boss does, what intellectuals do, what a father or a mother does, etc.

His first months of analysis were spent on detailed reports about his personal difficulties in making professional decisions – not just especially troublesome ones, but all kinds. He presented the problem and jumped to his own self-diagnosis: 'See, I am an indecisive person. A very indecisive person', he repeats, as if trying to convince him and me of this. This comment is immediately followed by a wishful thinking, self-reassuring statement: 'You know, as a psychiatrist, that it is normal to be ambivalent in my profession. Anyone in my job would be indecisive. I have to take decisions that involve millions of dollars. They always involve my own job, my own earnings.' Often he brought in memories from childhood. When he was a teenager, he tried to emulate his older brother, who was an outstanding pupil and good at sports. His brothers and sisters he describes as very successful; he insists on how good his family and origins are; he knows his genealogical tree from the eighteenth century, a rarity in Brazil. It was remarkable how good this man was at splitting off his painful experiences and feelings.

The sessions were filled by such memories and I observed that he was motivated by a prejudice: he was convinced that psychoanalysts would be happy to hear stories about the patient's childhood. Contradictorily, he nourished suspicions about 'this business of psychoanalysis which deals with traumas one had when one was a child. Psychoanalysis was deeply regarded in New York, London and Stockholm, but today's scientists know well that all of this talk is just bullshit.' Some sessions were spent on something he read about advances in drug therapy, about the physical nature of his illness – even though he said that it was not an illness, it was 'normal, as the psychiatrist from Europe said. See, it is genetic. My father medicated himself; he was his own doctor.'

Eventually – after six months – he finally noticed that I did not make queries. He became baffled with his own observation. 'But you never asked me about my childhood.' I noticed that he did not ask why; and that his concluding remark was almost emotionless, with the exception of a mild surprise, which thinly disguised a distant complaint – as if I were doing a kind of 'wrong psychoanalysis'. 'You know, I am afraid of falling prey to a third world professional, an untrained one. Thank God you were recommended by a trustworthy friend of mine. Well, no questions, again? I notice that you do not write when I come here, I never saw your notebook. Where is it? You take notes after the session? You have a very good memory!' Sometimes he would get up from the couch to see if I was writing or not. After having related some memories, he would ask, 'Have you no comments about my childhood? Be free to ask, I will answer!' Despite this type of comment, he tried to please me in things that he thought would be pleasing to me – or rather to his fantasy about me, as a man that would like to be pleased.

I thought that his surprise was due to the serious difference between what he thought ought to happen in the session and what really happened. It seemed strange to him that I tried to focus on the here and now, to describe and comment on what he was doing there, and what we were doing there. Emotional experiences emerging from our time together seemed to him pure nonsense.

After seven or eight months his initial bafflement was replaced by signs of interest which seemed to me genuine. He stopped making his thinly disguised complaints (which he saw as constructive suggestions) about the frequency of sessions, such as 'Perhaps I'll come twice a week now – is it really necessary to come here four times a week?' I hypothesised that I was dealing with a man who was hesitant in give up his prejudices, in stepping into what was unknown to him. From now on, I regarded all this talk about physical causes versus psychological causes as an epiphenomenal manifestation: a mere concrete, sensuously apprehensible appearance that presented a man full of prejudices. It seemed to me as not relevant in itself.

Time allowed me to observe that what was presented by him as 'indecisiveness' was not quite this: once more, it seemed to me just an appearance pointing to something beyond, even though it was not possible for me to fathom the underlying fact. After all, he seemed to me a real expert in his professional area, and I came to this conclusion not from his propaganda or manifest statements about it. Quite the contrary, he seemed to be a low profile man. Could the 'indecisiveness' have a paradoxical function, both pointing to and concealing something fundamental about the patient, like Freud's 'manifest content'? Was he dreaming that he was indecisive, or daydreaming, or was it pure hallucinosis?

Step by step, and slowly, a configuration emerged from his incidental, brief and scattered comments rather than his deliberate statements. For example, I learned that he quite often sought external help or advice from older professionals or leading figures in other firms. In fact he was baffled when his peers or, even more, younger people took action without doing so, since he believed such experienced opinions to be more authoritative, despite also judging some of these consultants to be 'arrogant'. His partners on the board supported his methods, though sometimes he used this search for external advice as proof of his indecisiveness: he would replace his characteristic 'See', 'You know', etc., with sheepish direct queries such as 'Do you think that I should do this?', then his typical patronising tone would return, slightly subdued. As far as I could see, it was owing to advice from one of these external consultants that he came to my consulting room. It then appeared that his successful, talkative, ostentatious father had undergone a long depressive episode. Then the picture of his mother changed from being a distant figure to one who showed a clear preference for his brother and sister, who now appeared not as highly successful but as disturbed and suffering from 'psychosomatic illnesses'. Much later he said his older brother, until then a kind of idol to him, had made more than a dozen attempts at analysis as well as having had at least twelve wives; he never acknowledged that he had a son, and refused to take care of the boy and much less to pay for his education.

Giulio seemed to have eruptions of sincerity, because his earlier reports about his own professional career – until now, a continuous upward climb – were gradually changing. He endured many failures. He nourished the idea of endorsing a great humanitarian cause, and aspired to fame. He also wanted to be very rich, 'to contribute to the development of our country, which is overwhelmed by famine and lack of education.' His political opinions seemed to me more appropriate for a teenager, despite his dealings with professional and rather high profile politicians. Juvenile hopes and despairs scattered throughout his ideas and aspirations.

When we met, his wife was in the last two months of her latest pregnancy. The complete absence of references to this was remarkable. I only heard about the delivery two months later, and even then he did not mention the sex of the child or the physical state of either.

He used to take his sons to amusement parks or on bicycle rides during the very few weekends he spent at home – most of them he was travelling abroad. He did this based on a sense of duty, and again it seemed that emotional experiences other than this were absent, or at best invisible, to him and to me. When he finally began to speak about his own family (as distinct from his family of origin, which he thought was what a 'correct' analysis was based on) I had the impression of an uncle or stepfather, a theatrical imitation of a real father, apparently amiable but ill-humoured at heart.

Clinical illustration

After having given some general ideas about him, I would like to quote in more detail a clinical illustration based on the last one. On this occasion he came grumpily to the session, even if with his usual overtly polite, smiling demeanour.

> He lies down, makes polite references to the weather, air-plane timetables, traffic conditions. I observe his underlying uncomfortable mood. He stops and says 'Oh, that's ok', distributing smiles as he turns his back, trying to look at me, in an awkward posture. 'I am fine, but you are right, I had a problem with my wife. She didn't give me enough bread for breakfast and kept shouting at me, saying it was my fault.' I could not understand exactly what he was saying – did she scold him out of the blue, or did he scold her first? He was silent. So I asked him about the two alternatives. 'No, no, no. I did not scold her. She was angry with me.' I was in the dark but I tried again: 'Could you tell me what happened? There was nothing to eat?' 'No, no. I ate the two remaining French rolls.' I noticed that his usual 'See ... you know ...' was replaced by a 'No, no', but the subdued tone made his angry mood almost imperceptible, but I sensed a menacing emotional climate, as if he meant: 'No, stupid!'
> It took us more time and a few other questions from me – because I knew that the family usually had breakfast together – to confirm an ensuing hypothesis that the children had nothing to eat. Still, he did not declare this explicitly, but just said his wife complained as usual, saying he was an egoist who did not care if he had a family or not. 'You

know, I had to go the airport.' I asked if he was late, and he said no, he had plenty of time; nor were his sons late. But he had no second thoughts about putting his own breakfast before that of his family, and felt victimised at not being granted favourite status. I notice that his usual way of speaking, 'You know…', strikes again, replacing the 'No, no', and that he refers just to the boys, but not to the girls.

He became anxious and persecuted when I asked those questions and invited him to think about those facts under a different vertex. Nevertheless, we were able to fathom that his ambivalence in terms of taking decisions expressed a fantasy of entertaining a passive function when he was relating with other males. He seemed to seek out a state in which he enjoyed the experience (in hallucinosis) of being penetrated by a man. This hypothesis, based on what he said about his father, the older brother, the Jewish friend at high school, and the 'consultants' (including how he found his way to analysis), confirmed by the way he sought my advice, displayed problems with his masculinity. He refused to look for women in the consulting enterprises and also displayed serious difficulties in putting forth his real opinions in a sincere way on any issue; every kind of disagreement was met with smiles and evasion. His behaviour in the session provided further evidence: if he had to miss a session – which he often did it, owing to his travels – he would postpone the announcement of his intention for as long as possible, or merely insinuate it in between other disparate comments.

My hypothesis now began to take account of his idea that he was a victim of 'panic syndrome'. Was the crisis of acute anxiety a manifestation of homosexual fantasies, which he unconsciously feared might emerge? During the sessions, he displayed a mixture of attempts at sheepish contact with me and of refusal of contact, in the form of covert misgivings about analysis as well as his difficulty in being sincere: would it result in a live manifestation of his homosexual fantasies? Moreover, it became evident that his manner of leaving the earlier job was not as simple as first described – in fact that now sounded more like propaganda. To keep his post he had to expand his staff and also to fire some others. He felt unable to do this, even though he insisted that none of those people were reliable workers. This all took place at the time when his best friend died (only now was it revealed that he had a 'best friend'). This friend was homosexual and Giulio had had a close relationship with him for more than twenty years, since student days: 'He was my friend, my confidant, my main adviser in everything'. He said he felt guilty because he did not visit his mother after his death, which it then appeared, from various details, was most likely a case of suicide.

The session after that of the 'breakfast' and of the complaining against his wife was taken up with accounts of his submissive behaviour before men he felt as 'intellectually stronger than him'. In that session, I tried to help him to face his homosexual fantasies in the way he was experiencing this fact in the here and now, when he asked for my advice when he had to take a particular action. As usual, he thought it impossible and rationalised: 'You know, you are a psychoanalyst, and for this reason, you must advise me, you know people, you know better'; and passed on to report another fact. It was characteristic that he would always try to turn any comment or observation of mine into a piece of judgement or advice; and if I remained silent he would feel this as evidence of disapproval or disavowal; so I always took care to refrain from making judgements about the truth of his stories and to wait for evidence from within the here and now of the session.

The next day I go to fetch him from the waiting room. This time, by contrast with his usual habit, he does not spend time bowing compliments but hurriedly enters the consulting room and lies down.

> After a few minutes in which he sits on the couch, staring at the wall and avoiding looking me in the eye, he lies down awkwardly, making disjointed movements with his hands until he finally combs his hair with them. He spent the next minutes on generalities. Nevertheless, this session lacked any of his usual preparatory movements before his lying down. Then he announces that he had a dream (though 'you know, I never dream'): *He was lying on a wheeled stretcher, in the emergency room of a large hospital. He had never seen this hospital. Hurried passers-by stopped, looked at him in horror and*

*shouted warnings: 'You are in danger! Beware! Someone shot you
in the neck, your legs will be paralysed – look out for the bullets!'*
'What in hell I was doing there, Dr Sandler? I am reminded
that I wanted to avoid the worst so I kept paralysed, immovable, see? And then I thought that everything was weird. I
tried to touch my neck with my own hand.' At this point he
touches his neck with his right forefinger. Overwhelmed by
emotion, he slightly rises in the couch – something new in
our experience in the session – as if he was trying to show
me: 'See, no blood, there is no blood either in me or in the
stretcher.' His anxiety increases. He repeats the hand-move-
ment many times – perhaps half a dozen – making increas-
ingly wider movements with his arms, as if trying to assure
himself that he could move. He then covers his hair with his
hand, touches the pillow with the palm of the same hand, as
if he were looking for blood. So in the dream, *he decided to
rise from the stretcher, arguing to the people around that he was
not shot, and walked away from the hospital, relieved of fear but
thinking the whole business nonsensical.*

The dream and above all the non-verbal mode in which he
reported it helped me to modify some hypotheses I had made
about his personality. At that point, I saw his fantasies as having
just a sexual nature, but the dream seemed to point to the existence of pregenital fantasies, kaleidoscopically amalgamated in
unstructured ideas of being pierced which could not be exactly
homosexual fantasies. For example, the paraplegia idea could
suggest impotence, but I found myself uneasy about such an
interpretation, which seemed to ignore other images within the
dream. Would it better to consider the emerging psychic fact
as confusion? There were people vouching that he was hit, he
was shot; and he was convinced that he was not, at least after a
moment of paralysing fear. This suggested he was in a state of
doubt for a while but then the confusion became intolerable and
he entered into a mode more typical of the paranoid-schizoid
position, thinking along the lines of 'right or wrong'. He 'got
away' from the confusion of whether he was shot or not, rises
up, and goes out.

From the happenings in the session, it seems to me that he really was confused: he asks what he was doing there – was he hallucinating? It did not seem a matter of referring to me as his analyst as if he were being attacked or pierced from his back, as if the couch were the wheeled stretcher. This seemed too direct and mechanical a transposition, founded on rationalisation. In my experience, to realise the hallucinatory nature of certain experiences of the patient or of the analytic pair differs from collusion. The dream seemed to present a compact picture of many acted-out features: telling us he had only the cloudiest notion of being a man, and so was not sufficiently potent to take real rather than feigned care of his family, or to deal with his work colleagues with the necessary firmness.

I tried to talk to him about what I felt as an infantile curiosity, as if he were a child making sexual researches on his own body, a foretaste of potential masculine potency (putting his hands to his neck, etc), exercising his feminine intuition rather than being a man prey to homosexual fantasies (which is true of any person, irrespective of gender). Was he making attempts to discern what a vagina is (the searching for blood) and to discriminate it from the anal orifice? He searched his own back, as if in a half-dreaming state; his neck might be, to him, his anus. I felt I was witnessing a man beginning to be able to exercise his budding and fumbling masculinity (the search), even though after this brief contact he got out and went away, in his usual self-reassuring mode. Because the real fact is that we had a dream of which he could be reminded – until then an impossible fact.

After this session, in which he listens silently but attentively to my interpretations, nodding from time to time, he comes back for a week, before beginning again his usual cycle of missing sessions: he had to travel, or didn't have to, or 'Well, you know, I badly wanted to have that orthopaedic surgery on my knee, I couldn't walk, my wife had to bring me food and had no time to look after our new baby.' A month later, out of the blue, he returned to analysis one sunny day wearing shorts, t-shirt and tennis shoes, looking like a teenager in the school holidays. He acts as if nothing had happened, makes no reference to the absentee sessions, but reports he is angry with the surgeon who told his wife the benefits of the surgery would only last a few months.

In the next session, he says he wonders why the technology of air-conditioners has not advanced in the last 40 years: 'A new, revolutionary technique would enable engineers to make machines that direct the flow to a specific point, thus would be energy-economising, or perhaps they could make another type which would spread the air more efficiently in wider areas.' I say he sees some advantages in growing, but he still sees growing from the vertex of pleasure. To him, adulthood is a phase when people are finally able to do only pleasurable things and may fulfil any wish they have. He agrees, as if I was defending such an attitude, and adds: 'Curious. I am reminded of a dream. It was very confused. *There is a very beautiful place on 65th Street. It is a store. It is a very elegant store: not luxurious, but elegant. It is in New York, you know, a very elegant city. I want to go inside – but what people would think about me, a man entering into a women's store? Well – thinking better, perhaps people would think that I would want to buy some clothes for my wife. But how they would know that I have a wife? You will see* (laughing), *the store has a funny name!* (laughs) *The Forgotten Woman. Well, in the dream, I enter and buy many clothes, the sales person rejoices.*

'Then I woke up and laughed a lot' (he laughs), 'because I was reminded of another store, on 45th Street. I would never buy things there! They sell badly made clothing, only for men. I think the clothes are made in Cuba or Nicaragua; it is called The Big Tall Man'.

Supervision

There is a rather long silence in the room; some colleagues are restless, making collateral conversations, in pairs. Dr Meltzer takes his time with tranquillity, turning the pages of the report, reviewing some parts and seems pensive, looking alternately up to the ceiling and to the pages. He utters to himself, but audibly, 'Interesting guy, this one'. And reads some pages again. Then he takes the microphone and says to the audience and also to me:

Donald Meltzer: There are some patients … you cannot believe in what they say. Not because they are liars, but because they try to deceive themselves. Most of them are just failures, because they do not arouse trust, and they are seen as liars, boasters, exhibitionists. This man attributed those qualities to his father, but at the same time he is intrigued that his father was successful. He gives me the impression – and the analyst may confirm my impression – that the success of his father was a pure Brazilian phenomenon, and that he does not want to risk emulating such a success. This patient seems not to perceive that the success of this father was a Brazilian phenomenon because he was able to adopt a Swedish professional persona.

In a certain way, despite Giulio's determination to not repeat his father's personality configuration, he does in fact repeat it, in a more intense way, because he possesses a more complete Swedish persona than his father ever had. As a consequence, he not only feels himself the ever-failing man, but also suffers from the permanent expectation of being discovered, of being humiliated. This man, who never dreamt in his life, finally brings some dreams, and begins to dream in analysis. It seems to me that he overcame his deeply denied but intense anti-semitism in relation to his analyst. His relationship to the analyst is in fact an intense one, founded in my view on the refusal of the analyst to deviate from the transference situation and go instead, for example, into an examination or speculation about the patient's past, or into his relations with people outside the session.

The analyst, in maintaining this position – which I consider the analytic position – placed himself in the position of challenging all the aspects of the personality and character of this man, rather than examining those aspects from the point of view of development. The analyst examined those aspects from the operational point of view of transference. This involves, in my understanding, an investigation into the trustworthiness of all the mental functions of the patient – beginning with the patient's ability to observe, to exercise his attention, to think, to communicate, to love, and to have sexual love. In this process the analyst discovered, to the patient's great surprise, signs of an intense femininity, the latent homosexuality, the transvestism and the patient's powerlessness to love a woman.

But I think that the analyst must not be satisfied with the acknowledgement of those defects. It would be better to handle those defects as facts in the development of the patient. The analyst must try to set the defects within a scale of development. I suppose they must be placed back at the beginning of adolescence, when the patient realised how impressive was his growth in height, which allowed people to deal with him as if he was unmistakably a male; thus his femininity turns into 'the forgotten woman'. I think it important that physical attributes evoke strong emotional reactions in other people, who bestow labels on a particular person, as a form of stereotype which practically functions as a fantasy. Therefore a kind of armour is imposed on the person's character which they may not even wish to avoid, because this armour also carries, at least in part, a social success.

This man escaped from being a stereotyped, starring sportsman, because he was not successful enough. I suppose he also escaped from being a rich and famous artist, probably because had little or no aptitude for it whatsoever. But what he swallowed socially made him a perfect social stereotype: he turned into a wealthy business administrator, a good manipulator – that is, he swallowed his father as a public figure. He was helped to attain this stereotype because he is tall and, I presume, handsome, as well as being a polyglot. In post-war times, to be a polyglot is a socially valued feature; it almost guarantees social success in the world of business – especially in the big business world.

Then it really impressed me how this analyst has persevered in taking this man so seriously, because this man is a deceiver, he is a highly successful fraud, and thus I imagine it must have been a huge countertransference problem not to throw him out. It must have been very hard to face this patient's pseudo-scientific, anti-analytic posture, to be kept in the shadow of a never openly expressed contempt. All of this must have generated a temptation to send him away. It is easy to treat patients like this who have attained such a degree of insincerity as if they were psychopaths. It is easy to say that they come to analysis not only to waste your time, but also to do you harm. And if they are as intelligent as they seem to be, owing to their gift for speaking many languages, they can also be dangerous seducers, who feign cooperation with you and with the analytic situation; but when they are outside the session, they ridicule psychoanalysis. The psychopath, for example, has a special gift for finding your other patients, in order to wound them through seduction and corruption. When a psychopath enters a training group, he is able to make it a real hell. I imagine that you may develop the impression that this man is a psychopath, that he is in analysis with the intention of doing harm. Nevertheless, I personally doubt that this is the case. I can see that this eruption of dreams allowed the analyst to pay attention to the sexuality of this man, to the balance between his femininity and masculinity. I can also see that his dream of having been shot in the neck and discovering there was no blood, could lead to the hypothesis that the dream has to do with anus, vagina and so on.

Anyway, I think that the most important thing is to concentrate on the ability of this patient to think when he is making his own observations, by contrast with the impact made by the opinions of other people – as you, Dr Sandler, show consistently in your way of conducting the analysis. Both ways of thinking emerge in that dream of being shot in the neck, and in the dream of the beautiful store on 65th Street, The Forgotten Woman, which is compared with a bad one on 45th Street, The Big Tall Man. It also becomes clear that those dreams have to do with fashion, and how large is the impact of fashion on this man, and also on his capacity to think. To him it is emotionally decisive if something is expensive and if a thing is placed in an elegant part of the city like 65th Street or in an ugly part like 45th Street.

This man offers a perfect opportunity for examination of his difficulty in thinking from his own observation, in that little episode about air-conditioning machines: he asks, why do engineers carry on making air-conditioners the same way they did 40 years ago? That is, in the time of his father. Surely a new revolutionary technique could be invented to make machines direct the airflow to a specific point, 'thus would be energy-economising, or perhaps they could make another type which would spread the air more efficiently in wider areas.'

All these are clichés, issued with neither knowledge nor comprehension: revolutionary technique, direct flow, energy-economising, bla-bla-bla. I would read this material as if it were a dream, a dream about the emotional relationship between people, in which new and revolutionary techniques are, fundamentally, the techniques of psychoanalysis. The revolutionary success is the mode which favours communication, instead of favouring actions, and how emotions can be directed to a specific point in other people, in order to enable communication with them.

In our situation, as analysts, the emotional climate between two people must be contained within tolerable limits, in order to allow for a continuous contact. This is the enabling effect of the psychoanalytic method, that tells you that you must observe the emotional state of the other person. The patient cannot do this when having dinner with friends, and cannot do this when he is in bed with his wife. He cannot do this in his professional activities, because he has no psychoanalytic methodology to scrutinise his countertransference, which would accustom him to retain such an ambience: of a communication-facilitating, tolerable and agreeable climate. You also have to observe your own emotional state. This kind of observation, as Bion taught us, makes thinking possible, because in a mysterious way, this is what allows for symbol-formation and dream formation.

Therefore, while I admire Dr Sandler's use of the analytic method, I also perceive that the presenter is trying to use the analytical method to deal with symptoms, as for example, the sexuality of this man. It is a huge temptation, especially for a man, to wish to put down this tall, large man who has involved the analyst in his stereotyped armour of a successful business-man, and to enable this man to get in touch with that forgotten woman, blind as he is to some bisexual state unintegrated internally. It is a huge temptation, in the light of the psychoanalytic history, to pay attention to analysing his psychopathology. Nevertheless, the analytic method demands that the analyst analyse just the mental processes. That was Bion's revolution:

to analyse the patient's capacity to think. The way to do that is exactly the one followed by the presenter when he demonstrates to the patient his own capacity to think, based on his capacity to observe the transference and countertransference.

Now, he rewards you, when he begins to dream. It is very tempting to then make exhaustive examinations of the dreams. But one need not to wait for dreams to employ the techniques of dream analysis. Everything that the patient says, that has signs of emotion, may be dealt with as if it was a dream. Everything that the patient says may be heard as if we were listening to a dream. The small passage about air-conditioning machines is a perfect example of what can be heard as if it was a dream, and may be treated as if it were an episode in symbol-formation. I believe – even though I am not absolutely sure – that the best way to do this is to utilise the visual imagination, because it is not mere coincidence that dreams are usually first presented as visual phenomena. Nevertheless, as you begin to see the visual formation of symbols, you will perceive the way that patients employ language to enlarge the symbolic loading of the visual. That is, we realise the use of jokes, of wordplay, of ambiguity, of slips of the tongue, that expand on the visual symbolism.

Paolo Sandler: I would like to express my gratitude for Dr Meltzer's generosity in his extended comments. This kind of supervision can expand the conditions under which one can view and understand one's patient. Dr Meltzer emphasised some aspects that are not in my report, but they correspond to my experience with this patient. For example, Dr Meltzer called this man a fraud, a fake. Yes, he acts and believes that he is an extremely seductive person, who really creates a pseudo-analytic, pseudo-collaborative atmosphere. I also thank Dr Meltzer for pinpointing the psychiatric vestige in my practice, that of focussing on the symptoms, at least in certain moments

I would like to ask two questions: the first is to know your ideas about the existence of a relationship, if there is one, between being gifted and the ability to dream? And, do you think that there is any method for discriminating dream from hallucination? To be more specific: is there any relationship between having an artistic gift and the ability of this artist to dream? Because there are people who imitate artists, that is, they are fakes, but they also are able to give concrete form to their hallucinations; and if one considers that artists also may give form to their dreams, would it be possible to state, based on the occurrences in an analysis, that a certain person lacked talent? I must add another comment on Dr Meltzer's discrimination, that there are patients who cannot be sincere, because they are not sincere with themselves. I suppose that this is not a judgmental, moral observation.

DM: I suppose that in the case of this man the idea of becoming an artist happened in the sphere of a social fantasy, in a way not so different from what happens when someone changes his job from an industry which makes the product X to go to another industry which makes the product Y. In other words, your patient could never become an artist because he had no passion for art. To an artist who displays a passion for art, it must be absolutely frustrating to witness the great success achieved by fake artists. It must be a real torture to be in love with a field which is in the hands of salesmen, gallery owners and art critics.

For people who love psychoanalysis, there is a similar problem, about which we will talk more at some future point, because the fashion which is represented by this man has a practically irresistible impact. This patient's description of his father – 'a typical South American macho' – could be applied to anyone who knows how to behave in a system ruled by fashion, regardless of the field. It seems to me that this man is a perfect example of someone with a major thinking disorder, typical of people of people whose incapacity to think is disguised or camouflaged by the fact that they are good talkers.

Such camouflage techniques, which I think this man illustrates, involve fashionable jargon as well as the clichés so effectively employed by politicians. As soon as they are confronted by the analytical investigation of their processes of thinking, and the need to produce analysable material, they display a wonderful talent for camouflage, which they do in a very special way, because we never can catch them with their hand in the cookie jar. One may study their methods by viewing any broadcast or TV political debate. They create a rhetorical background that answers all questions, as for example, 'This reminds me of a funny experience I had yesterday'; or they simply invent a story to fit that context; or they present statistics; or create their own statistics that dovetail to the context. A good trick is to use bits of sincerity. Fortunately, it is difficult to simulate sincerity. One recognises that when one is situated in another room listening to a political programme on radio or TV: no one would mistake it for a normal conversation; it is unmistakable the way they project their voices, as if they were on stage, being looked at and also looking at themselves. I find it lucky, that it is so difficult to pretend to be sincere. In the case of Giulio for instance, he clearly sensed his mother's inability to be sincere.

There was an intriguing thing in the beginning of this patient's analysis: he could not comprehend what was his analyst's method, because it did not coincide with any of the prejudices about the psychoanalytic method he had entertained until then. The truthfulness of the method wielded a huge power over the patient. He was unable to unveil Dr Sandler's thoughts. He depended on circumstances such as 'Thank God you were recommended by a trustworthy friend.' When his prejudices received no confirmation he became confused. From that point of view, the whole analysis illustrates very important questions: how does one begin an analysis and how does one establish an analytical situation? Anyone endowed with a good enough intelligence and culture comes to analysis worried about the analytical method. In the first days, weeks, months, and even years, those people bring a false transference, based on prejudices.

This prejudiced structure, as it were, must be disassembled. I call it a 'preformed transference'. It demands strenuous work to dismantle a preformed transference, in order to make room for the emergence of a true infantile transference. Dr Sandler already accomplished this part of the work, so the patient has encountered a workable transference. I want to emphasise that such a preformed transference differs from the transference that exist in borderline psychotics, whose lives are made of projective identifications.

Probably you had considered this patient as an example of pseudo-maturity, but he is in fact an example of an absolute lack of maturity, for he is imprisoned within a social armour, built around him on the grounds of his physical attributes, his parents' attitudes, his immersion in his cultural environment. I can see no use for the term 'immaturity' in this kind of patient. He is not immature, he is just a child. He illustrates a kind of phenomenon that can easily be seen in almost all six-year-old boys who are taller than their peers.

Participant: When an analyst tries to show the patient the preformed transference, does the analyst know what the infantile transference is?

DM: When you are faced with a preformed transference, it is necessary that you use your imagination about children. In this situation experience in working with children, or with your own children, can be indispensable; this being the case, you will not regard those patients as immature, but as children whose behaviour enacts their particular belief system.

CHAPTER SEVEN

Thought disorder from living in a claustrophobic world
(1991)

Marisa Pelella Mélega

T he first presentation of the case of Marie was in 1991, in Oxford, and was followed up on Meltzer's visit to Uruguay two years later. Marie, 32 years old, had been in analysis with me for just over two years, with sessions four times a week. She had suffered from panic disorder for over 20 years, and had weekly support and reassurance therapy sessions for eight years. When she came to analysis she expected an immediate affirmation that psychoanalysis had been a good choice. At the consultation, she recounted a traumatic event that took place when she was two and a half years old when her parents left her and her eighteen-month sister in a Swiss school where no one spoke Portuguese for a period of two weeks. She believed this trauma lay behind her problems; her sister, she said, did not suffer in the way, as she was there to calm her down. She could not go out alone and was always in a hurry to return home; as a child she would not travel at weekends with her parents but stayed at home with a maid. She did not have a regular job, but would occasionally take on translation projects that she did at home. She was not paying for her analysis with her own money. She had recently developed a fear of contracting all kinds of diseases: imagining a simple cold to be pneumonia, a ganglion cyst to be cancer, or a mouth ulcer to be a sign of AIDS. Twelve years before coming to analysis she had abandoned a college course in Education six months before graduation: she had felt somewhat dizzy, unable to stand up on her own, and fearful of being in crowded places.

The beginning of analysis

Marie's parents drove her to my consulting room, even though they only lived two blocks away. Marie described her panic states and obsessive concerns. She showed great verbal ability in describing her feelings, saying she was 'absolutely aware of everything, but unable to change anything'. The counterpoint to this mental attitude was a sense of hopelessness and the impossibility of change, because she claimed the problem was beyond her control and that her suffering was constitutional.

Donald Meltzer: Panic is the past presented undigested, not thinking.

Marisa Mélega: I will describe two sessions from last year, to each of which she brought two dreams. At the first session, before lying down, Marie says that she wants to apologise for not being able to pay her fees that day when they were due; but that she will manage by the end of the week. I was surprised, as her manner suggested some more serious declaration, such as a decision to discontinue the analysis. I told her that flexibility is part of the analysis and I understood she really wanted to show her thanks for the session (it was a substitute time) by being able to pay me.

Marie says her mother stayed with her while her father went with her sister to Maresias (a village on the cost): 'I am calmer, although I feel a little embarrassed, guilty, because she stayed behind.' I comment on her fear of controlling me, as if I were there, seeing her in analysis, as a result of her control over me. She did not notice the fantasy and seemed to be distant.

She recalled two dreams, then, from the previous two nights. The first dream: *On the other side of the street I see a church, a party, music. I cross over and inside the church is the pastor and another man, and I think I'm going to dance with him, but the one who asks me is a horrible fat woman. I think – dance with this person? I make an excuse that I have to go because the baby is crying and I rush home. The door is old with a rather rusty handle that is almost loose, and I close it carefully to prevent the fat woman from coming in. Inside the house is a horrible uncle of mine of whom I've always been scared, and my father and my mother are there quarrelling (which never happens in real life) and she tells me to keep calm, that I am not guilty of what is happening.*

The second dream: *I was in the street with a group of colleagues from the university; I was in a hurry to return home; I had to take a taxi, but there weren't any. We thought about taking a bus – can I stand it? We walked along Santo Amaro Avenue, but suddenly there are road works with enormous pipes in the street, and beside them heaps of people, dead and dying from illness. I think about not going that way, in order to avoid contamination, but I am already there and I go on, always running, everything in a rush, because of the anxiety of having no time.*

Marie associates her dream to being in the supermarket and taking a pen to sign her name; at this moment she was caught, as if she were stealing the pen; she did not know how to prove that she was not stealing the pen, but was simply using it to sign her name. I take note of her very severe self-criticism of her failures and hostile feelings.

To a session three months later, Marie brought these two dreams: *I am at a school, ugly, dark everywhere and enclosed. I act as if I am a superhero, a wonder-woman; I make it rain; a light rain falls. Everyone applauds; but my mother does not pay any attention to me, as if all this means nothing to her.*

In the second dream, she says: *I don't remember why my mother is scolding me.* She also remembers dreams from a few days before when *there was a scorpion inside the sofa on which she was seated,* and another in which *she opened a tap and a rat came out.* I remind her how she feels criticised when I broach her defences.

DM: This patient presents pseudo-maturity, through the projective identification part of her personality with its arrogance, self-consciousness and omnipotence. Her identity is based on how other people see her; many times she dreams she is acting. Patients like her are unable to be sincere. They don't have a concept of sincerity. They don't have an idea of their emotions, and emotion is consequence of behaviour, for example, if one has intercourse one falls in love. She lives in a claustrophobic world.

MM: At another session four months ago, Marie came in saying: 'I am feeling somewhat tired, I'm worried I have a heart condition, I went to make my bed and got out of breath – what is the point? It got me thinking that if I do have a heart condition, what point is there in doing what I am doing? If I was sure I didn't, I would be able to get a grip, to stop worrying about it. But, if I do, and I let it go, what will happen? So, I have to keep looking after myself.'

In another session she again complained of distress and of shortness of breath while watching TV without having exerted herself, and she also said she had colitis. I talk about the imaginative life with which she has no contact: she has no awareness of it, yet it has an effect on her body. She related a dream, a nightmare (explaining she had lived at her grandmother's house for eight months after she came back from the United States with her family): *I was at my grandmother's house, it was all dark and ugly and there was a threat of an invasion. Outside, in front of the house, were some boys on bikes; I wanted to shout, to frighten them away, but no sound came out.* (She says that in fact, it is usual for her to dream that her voice won't work.) *It seems that my father is coming in, through the back of the house. I don't know if there was a maid or not. Later on, animals come out through the back – ducks, etc. I continued to feel threatened.'*

Her associations were of being anxious about the impending break in the analysis. I told her that in the dream she seemed to be living the impending separation: she seemed to be in transit, going out of the place with the animals to a closed (but not so safe) and dark place (the breathlessness she complains about) with her belongings (in the dream, they are the radio, handbag, etc.), but this was a gathering of her emotional belongings that would stay with me – through the approaching threat in the external world (children on bikes referring to the personal life of the analyst). Her voice won't work. What will the analyst do, who takes away her psychoanalytic sessions?

DM: She cultivates the production of these thoughts. One part of her personality is in a massive projective identification and the other part is free from it. You need strategies to work with her: describe the internal world that she experiences and try to disconnect the ill part (in projective identification) from the healthy part. This is the nature of a claustrophobic world. The psychotic part seeks company, so she takes you inside the claustrophobic world. The fundamental idea is that she lives in a closed world and the outside world is dangerous, but you must show her that what she thinks is the outside world is in fact a compartment of her own inner world.

Progress of the analysis

Meltzer had also emphasised the confusion between self and object in her projective identification: she did not accept their separateness. Her thoughts were concrete, with confusion between the symbol and the symbolised.

Over the next two years Marie gave more evidence of her entrenched thought disorders. At times I commented to her that she presented defences against psychic pain, in order to sustain her conflicts. Why was she unable to work through conflicts and seek for the resolution of mental pain? She felt she had been ruined, been damaged by her sister, who had all her parents' affection. When I showed her the transformations she made, for example, she argued, denying them and concluding with her hope that something could be done, leading me to exasperation because of the irreducibility of her ideas and for twisting what we had talked about: always leading me to the same dead end. I understood her need to make me feel concerned, but she left me without an escape route in the face of so much madness.

She talked about her obsessional rituals intensifying and her difficulty in concentrating: how she needed to worry in order to concentrate but at the same time she then became too scared that something bad would happen. This was her worry in relation to her physical or psychosomatic symptoms and also in relation to anything else, such as her father being absent on a trip.

At one period she seemed more receptive, apparently listening to me and refraining from strongly attacking what I would say. Her belief in the analytical process seemed to be growing, or perhaps it was that her steadfast disbelief and despair were eroding. When the long vacation approached both she and I were concerned about the prolonged interruption (though she referred more to her parents' absence than to the analysis) and we had several family meetings; she ended up accepting the possibility of having someone accompany her when she goes out, or to keep her company; someone who is not necessarily a family member. But then her symptoms seemed to worsen: she vomited at night and panicked, terrified of dying, resulting in an extra session where she attacked me for not giving me my home number in case she wanted to contact me at the weekend. I explained that we had agreed I was going to be her analyst and that, if she is undergoing analysis, it is because she is able to be an analytic patient – and this type of patient does not need to see the analyst over the weekend.

In the course of the next year she continued with her panic syndromes, which we were able to link with her fear of the emotions arising from relationships, and she seemed to recognise this difficulty, in the context of re-reading an old diary from her teenage years which made her realise she had suffered from fears for a long time, and her panic syndrome had not suddenly developed out of nowhere.

In one session she presented two dreams. The previous week she had been constantly attacking me with paranoid and pre-established arguments since the week before. In the first dream, *she is looking for her grandmother's house. When she gets to the place, the house is not there.* In the second, *she is in a car together with her father and sister. The car runs out of control, but her father and sister do not realise it. The road is full of cars and it looks like they are going to crash. The situation leads her to take control of the car, even though she is really scared. Everything is out of control, but she manages to stop the car by driving it against an embankment.*

Two months later she recounted a dream that she associated with an orphanage she had visited and with the Swiss school whose details she describes and remembers visually. In the dream: *There was a big, dark bedroom full of little beds. It was like an orphanage and I was lying on a bed and taking a test. There were American nurses there and I was nervous, because my parents went away and I called out 'Mum!' I wanted to know where they were going, when they would come back. I had to take the test. I was taking the test, but I ran out of paper and I wanted more paper to go on writing … then my parents appeared … it seems there were mountains.'*

Donald Meltzer: She talked about the orphanage dream as if it were a reconstruction of her relationships with her mother and sister and her toilet training.

Marisa Mélega: Imagine her experience, when she was two, at the Swiss school: evacuating her faecal contents without knowing who they were destined for; without knowing who would reassure her from her dread of bad contents.

The following year

She continued with her somatic complaints and her parents became desperate about her lack of progress. She said, 'Hope is just a wish, it is the Promised Land! I just know I cannot take it anymore.' At one point she had some dreams which I found more promising: one in which *she was locked in the kitchen, forgotten by her parents and sister, but screamed so that a neighbour could hear her.* In another, *a woman was about to give birth and she was trying to help her and to contact her husband to say she could take her to hospital.* I hoped these dreams were signs of a desire to free herself from her imprisoned world and to be born into reality. I commented: 'You cannot take being locked up anymore.' Some months after that she spoke of being terribly afraid without knowing what she feared. She cried, saying she did not know if she was scared of living or dying. I told her that she had reached the point of not knowing, while before, she knew everything, but was unable to change anything. But this was progress – even if she was disturbed by this state of mind.

The following material was presented to Meltzer at an event in Montevideo, Uruguay, in 1993.

Marie had started the session by telling me she had spent the entire week crying: that I moved to a new office in order to get rid of her, which was a serious setback for her and she did not know how she would find someone to drive her to the new office.

I reminded her we managed to find more favourable times for her sessions and that her sister offered to drive her to my consulting room – that everybody had cooperated. Her reply was: 'Well, the discomfort of getting here from home is still a problem for me.' She then started to tell me how concerned she was about having AIDS, because an ulcer appeared in her mouth and she had read that a common way to be infected with HIV is going to the dentist, and she went to the dentist the month before. She also mentioned that December is coming and everybody will be on vacation, including me, and she will have to go to the beach with her parents for the Christmas holidays even though it would be torture for her but she could not refuse to go again as she did last year, which forced her parents to stay at home.

I asked her what she was doing to prepare for this 'battle'. She said she was doing nothing except praying to escape death and that she hates everything about the beach: the sand, mosquitoes, the mess – nothing makes her happy. She wished things were as they had been in the past when she was normal. I ask what used to make her happy in the past, and she answers that it is no use wasting time with this kind of thing. I suggest it is a waste of time thinking hypothetically about unpleasant possibilities such as AIDS but she denies this vigorously because of the 'reality' of the mouth ulcer. 'I can never go back to what I once was', she complains.

I point out it is harder for her to talk about the things she would like and to have good thoughts than to tell me she thinks she has AIDS. She said it would be good if she could plan and make things, or if I gave her some hope. The conversation then went as follows:

Patient: You don't tell me if I can be cured of this terrible panic, so what's the use of asking me what I would like to do? It is the same thing as asking what Marcelo Rubens Paiva [a famous Brazilian writer and host of a television show, who is disabled] would like to do if he could walk, and he would say that he would like to play football, go swimming …

Analyst: You give an example of someone who is physically disabled; but you confine yourself to your home, you are afraid to go out, yet say you feel like him.

Patient: He does not confine himself; I even envy him, because he is there, on TV, doing everything; and the mere fact that I am comparing myself with him doesn't mean that I have to put up with the idea of being disabled.

Analyst: This is a distortion. You brought the comparison.

Patient: But, you took advantage of it!

Analyst: I took the opportunity to show you that, although this person is now unable to play football, he can do other things. But you didn't want to hear what I said; you saw me as accusing you.

Patient: Because I only wanted someone to reassure me that my case is not the same as his.

Analyst: You wanted to be sure! No human being is sure of anything – that I can tell you.

Patient: Why can no one be sure of anything? I wanted to be sure I will be totally cured. I want to be well.

Analyst: I wonder why you cannot tolerate doubts, yet manage to live well.

Patient: I can't …

Analyst: That's it. You can't cope with conflicts.

Patient: No! Marcelo Rubens Paiva maybe has conflicts. Who knows, maybe he will be able to walk again; I don't know how …

Analyst: Well, you have another problem! Up to now, people are sure that he will not be able to walk again.

Patient: My problem is also walking, I have a mental problem, but it is also related to walking. I want you to promise that, if I make an effort, if I do this or that, I will be well again.

Analyst: This is such a strange thought.

Patient: So, you mean I have to put up with it?

Analyst: It is a very strange thought: you want to build another reality –a reality where you can be sure all the time. But, in spite of everything, there is no reality made of certainties.

Patient: It's like telling Marcelo Rubens Paiva: 'This is the best you can have. So, put up with it and try to live your life as it is.'

Analyst: You want me to say something like that to you. You think, for example, that someone who is going to make an archaeological investigation will only do so if he is sure of what he is going to find. You are telling me that you won't do anything unless you are sure you will find the treasure. Then, you just don't do anything at all.

Patient: It is different! You are talking about archaeology. I am alive ...

Analyst: You say you need to be sure, to start cooperating. So, what should we do?

Patient: You give the impression that you don't believe I will be cured.

Analyst: I think you are the one who does not believe you can be cured.

Patient: Otherwise, you would have said something to encourage me.

I went on to discuss the way she would only look at one part of the problem and ignore the overall picture. We had already talked about her despair and her desire for me to perform a miracle; that I had to defend her against all the bad thoughts she constructs. She demanded a continuous verbalisation of good thoughts in order to neutralise bad thoughts. I could not tell her whether she could be cured, but often told her she was making progress, listening more, feeling the need to 'put her house in order' through the analytical work. She would look scared and say she had always been like that, which confused me.

Patient: You never assure me that I will be completely cured.
Analyst: And what do you mean by 'completely cured'?
Patient: To go back to what I once was.

Analyst: A few minutes ago, we saw that you were unable to tell me what you were like, what things you liked; you reveal yourself to be a sad person without hope. For you, everything is lousy, no one likes you, you don't believe in anything. Where is the other side of life? I know it exists.

Patient: There used to be one … but it has been destroyed.

Analyst: It still exists, and it is up to you to give it a chance by forgetting your resentment.

Patient: But you have to give me hope that I will be alright.

Analyst: Doesn't the fact that we are here, working together, serve to make you more hopeful?

Patient: But you don't tell me I will be alright. For example, if you break your leg and go to the doctor, he knows if he is able to treat it and if your leg will be all right.

Donald Meltzer: She induces a negative pleasure through her fantasies not becoming reality – this is the hypothetical exercise she indulges in, which prevents her from having experiences she can learn from. She makes up a story to avoid having experiences. She fabricates some story about what will happen and carries on saying what would have happened; her pleasure in living comes from what did not happen, from what is supposed to happen.

This is a part of a thought disorder with circular arguments. When she refers to the disabled television presenter, she claims not to be envious of his capacity to overcome his handicap. We can imagine a process in which the envy is split off, but I think that is not it. Instead I think it is an argument for why she should not feel envious of him, of his ability to overcome his handicaps: an argument for why she should not feel envious of being unable to overcome her handicap. It is a circular and confused thought process.

The person we are dealing with is different from a child or someone with a developmental disorder; we are dealing with someone with thought disorder. She is very argumentative. This is difficult, technically, but the arguments have to be worked through in order to reveal the thought disorders to her. It really is an arduous and unpleasant task to work with thought disorders, because, in my experience, these patients are extremely argumentative and unable to employ language for the correct reasons.

You are not just dealing with a 'spoilt baby', you are also dealing with a girl who cannot use her mind in a constructive manner, especially as she has wasted her time with this negative way of entertaining herself – by inventing catastrophic stories that never come true. This gives great pleasure if you see it in a film, because the risk of you experiencing it in reality does not exist.

Postscript

The night after I wrote the material for this seminar, I had the following dream: *Marie is with some other people, as if they were visiting a museum. I observe Marie's behaviour from a distance and am surprised that she is able to remain in this group: I see that she is more present in herself. Then I see her with a group of young people, sitting on the floor as if they were waiting for something. Someone offers her modelling clay and she accepts it. She begins working it with both hands and rapidly creates something that looks like a revolver, or perhaps a giant penis or a nipple. It is red, the colour of raw meat. Her movements are fast and assured, like an artist moulding a work of art. Then, she acts as if she were holding a gun and shooting repeatedly. The young people nearby ask her to stop it. She appears to listen to them.*

This dream, which, of course, also contains my personal input, does include my thoughts on Marie, especially her reconstruction of the breast-nipple-penis in a masturbatory fashion – her quick movements transform the combined object into a weapon that she wields with omnipotence, but she stops at the request of the young people in the dream.

CHAPTER EIGHT

Confusional states and a childish erotic transference
(1996)

Marisa Pelella Mélega

The case of Brigitte was first presented to Meltzer in 1996 at a supervision seminar in Sao Paulo. Seven years previously, I was sought by a 32-year-old woman who had a two-year-old son and was suffering intensely both in her role as a mother and within herself. Brigitte was a petite, good-looking brown-haired woman, who instantly expressed herself much more through emotional signs (anguished sighs, tone of voice, exclamations, loud laughter, scared glances) than verbally. She made it clear she had come for analysis for her own sake because she felt fragile and had great difficulty when faced with separations, frequently becoming desperate.

During the first year of analysis (with four sessions a week) she had a great need to talk about commonplace events, apparently without any great emotional content, until she would end up sobbing convulsively and shouting, completely changing track. Then she begged to relate very painful episodes in her life such as, for example, the fact that her father was in prison, or the death of her nanny, who died when she was eleven, and whom she viewed as her own mother. I would feel completely overwhelmed by the narrative, which rose to a crescendo until the explosion mentioned above, when I could crawl out from under the barrage and speak.

When beginning the sessions she would feel oppressed, and normally, at the end, leave relieved. She would feel hatred because I showed her that she was not in analysis simply for me to take care of her but so that together, we would try to understand her feelings and thoughts. Later, she succeeded in verbalising how she used to fight with me when I wouldn't 'take her on my lap' but instead told her that she was an adult who resisted working with her mind.

Donald Meltzer: Did she lie on the couch from the very beginning?

Marisa Mélega: Yes. She is capable of resolving things in reality. She is pragmatic, but doesn't value this capacity; she only values being pain- and anxiety-free, and thinks if there is pain or anxiety she is failing, and I am failing. Her will is sovereign. Her capacity to accomplish objectives, even to tolerate frustration, is not considered valuable. Separation from the external containing object (analyst) leads to frustration, hostility, and, at times, to acting-out. There is a little recognition of a psychological relationship; the analyst's prime quality is perceived to be her physical, sensuous presence.

A few months after the beginning of analysis, she came to a Monday session, saying that she wanted to die and she had fought against this feeling over the weekend, thinking of her son, then she burst into convulsive sobs. At the end of the first year of analysis, she brought two dreams, which showed, I thought, the intensive transference relationship with the analyst.

She began the session with lots of sighing, saying how difficult it had been to come today. She said that she had dreamt about the analyst on two occasions:

DM: Can we take one dream at a time?

MM: By all means. The first dream: *I was in this room, and in that corner* (pointing) *there was a standing lamp which looked like me, from which sparks began to fly, like a short-circuit. You turn it off, from time to time sparks erupt, and you unplug the lamp when I tell you that, even turned off, there was still a current. Then it seems that I am sitting, and you ask me if I want a fruit salad.* She associates this with my lamp, and says she likes fruit salad, made in various ways, and had made one at Christmas.

DM: This is a simple straightforward dream involving the analytical situation, its explosivity, as well as the desire for the relationship between her and the analyst to be pleasantly confusing. I take she is one of those patients who find confusion as a great relief, in the face of all situations demanding explanation and decision.

MM: The second dream: *It is this room, but the couch is against the wall with the window, and you tell me that one of your patients had said that there wasn't a window in this room. In the dream, I thought: but why is Marisa telling me this?'* She associates it with a supervisor who has a couch under a window.

DM: Again this is a simple dream involving the patient's quite strong desire for an analysis aiming at her outside life. But this desire reveals a problem of competitiveness with other patients who are more capable of dealing with the transference and countertransference situation in a contained way. Both dreams put together seem to indicate that the patient prefers her analysis to deal with her outside life. This reveals a preference for acting and the creation of a comforting confusion.

MM: In this same session she tells one more dream, saying she doesn't know exactly when it was. The third dream: *I was in this room, with a longer couch, and you are lying with your legs like this* (she shows me her open legs), *and I sit at your feet, leaning my arm there* (she shows me that it is a kind of support). *Then I embrace you, and we roll on the sand like two lovers.*

DM: Now you get the picture of the result of this preference for acting, which includes acting in the transference and turns the analytical situation into a love affair. The juxtaposition of her body and the analyst's body in the dream is done in such a way that the patient can look right into the analyst's genitals. And the patient prefers the analyst to invite her for this kind of relationship, in which the analyst constantly exhibits her genital activities to the patient. In the beginning this was called 'being taken onto the analyst's lap'.

The implication is that this kind of attitude exempts her from any competition with other patients. It implies a form of relationship between a mother and her baby, where the baby is treated as if it were a penis constantly excited by the mother, in a constant desire for intimacy and penetration – not necessarily to gratify such desire, but simply keeping the baby in a state of excitement. This is the patient's preference, and also the infantile orientation to be found in the transference, that is, to be this kind of baby with this kind of mother. On the surface, it seems to mean getting rid of the Oedipus complex, but in fact she is only apparently getting rid of it through this projective identification with a father's penis. It can be a reference to a kind of breastfeeding in which the baby – when sucking the nipple – provides the mother with more sexual excitement than the father provides in his genital relationship to the mother. Thus it is a reference to a type of breastfeeding which is more likely to be found with a little boy than with a little girl. It is the basis for the break-up of many marital relationships after the first baby.

MM: The first period of analysis is characterised by day-to-day fears of not controlling her life and her catastrophic anxieties; there are few free associations and dreams.

In the second year of analysis she experienced a new infatuation, and she began to speak about this complicated passage in her life, her tendency to fall in love, which seemed to me to represent an escape into another aspect of her functioning, which she calls 'a lead soldier': doing without wanting to feel. The infatuation turned into a threat to destroy everything she had (husband, son, profession), break up with everything.

Sometime later, Brigitte began to bring some dreams to the session, sometimes becoming ashamed of the contents that showed her infantile sexuality.

Progress of the analysis

Brigitte comes at a new time for the session today and I, the analyst, forget the new time. At this period she is having two sessions a day, on two days a week. I had cancelled the first session today.

Brigitte begins: 'You told me I felt threatened by the change of the session time, and I couldn't see it. But yesterday afternoon

I began to have pains and shivering spells. I went to bed early and woke at one in the morning feeling cold, with hot joints. Could it be arthritis? I thought. I took a painkiller and went to sleep. I dreamt that *I had come for the session, and you had told me that it was from 10 to 9, and that we would have three classes afterwards, and also that I would pay by cheque, I don't know from whom, but it appeared to be a school situation rather than our analysis.* I awoke thinking about this dream and afterwards slept again.'

DM: This is one of the incidents that illustrate what Freud meant about the transference being a repetition of the infantile situation. But what it demonstrates is that the transference is intended by the patient to repeat the story she has made in her mind about her childhood.

This episode in which the analysis seems more like a school situation has something to do with the infantile school situations in which she behaved in a very seductive way with her teachers and sought to place herself in a preferred situation, to be a 'pet'. It probably also has a certain reference to the way in which she exchanged her mother for the nanny, and behaved in a seductive way with the nanny which may or may not have been enacted. But the important thing, as indicated by the dreams, is to understand a part-object *voyeuristic* relationship in which her preoccupation with the genitals is given ample scope for realisation. For example, if a child is sleeping in a room with her nanny, she has plenty of opportunity to see the nanny's dressing and undressing, and so on.

The other thing worth mentioning is the way in which a patient like this feeds in this story of her childhood for the purpose of programming the analyst to interpret in a certain way. In this case, she would be seeking an interpretation about what a neglected child she was. And, of course, she shouldn't be fed by the electric current that produced the sparks and the explosions; she should be fed with the nice comforting fruit salad of confusion.

MM: We now have a session shortly afterwards where she brings the following dream: *I was seated on the couch and you laid your head on my lap. I am wearing a skirt; you lift the skirt, remove the panties and say to Dalva* (the nanny) *that the vitamin hadn't* *been put there (pointing to the clitoris), but here (pointing to the vagina). I became aroused.*

DM: It shows how any disturbance of setting is welcomed by the patient, because of the confusion that it generates. It is greeted by the patient as if the analyst were exhibiting her genitals. It means something like: any change of session time is experienced by the patient as if the analyst had said: 'Sorry, I can't feed you today because daddy insists on having intercourse with me; he is forcing me to do something that I don't want to, when I would much prefer for you and me to be masturbating one another.'

MM: The next week, she arrived saying that she was very distressed on the Wednesday after the Carnival holiday, but that now she is better, and thought that it was because of the change in the rhythm of the sessions. Then, she related two dreams. In the first, she describes *a table, full of objects that remind her of dead people, and she thinks they belonged to her nanny; they are paraphernalia, like the box for the hearing aid.* Then, she comments that the nanny was not deaf to her, and says: 'I am confused, because now I don't know if the person in my dream was my mother or the nanny.'

DM: Those are her precious moments of the confusion between mother and nanny. The thing that was so powerfully attractive for her was the evidence that her relationship with the nanny was exclusive, that it excluded her father and it excluded any siblings.

MM: The other dream: *You are dressed in beige crochet, and I am resting on your arm, your head covered with a crocheted hood. And I say that old love is better and turn around and kiss your arm, almost at the height of the armpit. Then you leave, and I calm down.* She says she woke up from this dream feeling well, and the anxiety she felt on Wednesday had gone.s

DM: It's very difficult to interpret the meaning of this beige crochet dress and the hood that she's wearing, but what is apparent is that this kiss in the armpit us really a genital kiss: near the armpit unquestionably means a genital kiss. This ancient love, old love. It is the kind of genital love that comes before the arrival of any new baby who can suck on the breast. It is as if to say: genital love comes first. Of course, if this were an acknowledgement that the parental genital love precedes the making of the baby, that would be fine. But it doesn't mean this. It means that the baby's earliest relationship to the mother in the womb is, in fact, an erotic relationship.

MM: This is a fragment from a session when she was still having two sessions a day and two on another day.

> I meet her in the waiting room, opening the bathroom door, and she makes a sign that she will come in shortly. So, I go and wait for her in the consulting room. She enters and remains silent for a long time. Then she says: 'It is difficult to talk. I feel that I'm changing, and I am satisfied with some of these changes, but with others, I don't know.'
>
> I suggest the possible change in her state of mind is perhaps related to the fact that we met each other in the waiting room. Then she makes the following association: her son is sitting on the toilet to do pooh-pooh and playing with an arrow; this arrow falls into the toilet and she tells the boy off. He then says that he doesn't want to do pooh-pooh any more.

DM: It looks as if she didn't like you seeing her come out of the bathroom. This is immediately felt as a reprimand of some sort.

MM: In the following session on the same day, she says, after lying down: 'I don't know if I recognise you when I see you. After I lie down, I hear your voice. I identify it as coming from you, and I calm down.'

DM: My reaction to this particular statement by the patient is that she feels embarrassed when she meets the analyst face to face because she feels that the analyst is reprimanding her for always looking up her skirt at her genitals. That is, we are getting very close to the patient acknowledging what you might call her 'dirty-mindedness'. She is constantly using the analyst to excrete her faecal and urinary thoughts. Of course, it's one of the pitfalls of baby care that when the mother cleans the baby's bottom (which means with a little girl also cleaning her genitals), the baby can experience it as a seduction. One of the devices that mothers use when they are cleaning the baby's bottom is to keep talking to distract attention from this erotic cleaning operation. But this can be experienced by the baby as an invitation to collude in denying the erotic relationship. It often happens in analysis that you have a patient who regularly uses the toilet that is made available to him, but never mentions it.

MM: We go on now to a session about eight months later, when she relates the following dream: *I was with my supervisor at home, in my consulting room, my brother was in my armchair* (where I usually sit to work), *my husband was in the waiting room, but his body was that of my father. We go out to the yard, and the supervisor transforms into a woman with a penis. She leans on my thigh, and I get excited. She says that she is going to teach me to use the penis; in the yard, she sits on a bench and takes me on her lap, kisses my breasts, and I look at hers, but think that she is old, and I want a younger breast. Now, I am in Rio de Janeiro, in an apartment building on the beach. A man wants to set up a food stall; I tell him not to put it in Copacabana, but in Ipanema. The waves start to enter the building, and I save the books. In the children's nursery there is an enamel jar with meconic* (poppy) *fluid inside.* (At this point she becomes emotional and starts to cry.) *And I ask myself if my son is alive; I see Cazuza* (the singer), *but before he contracted AIDS.*

DM: You are getting the whole picture of her realisation of the perversity of her erotic preoccupations in the transference, but you also get a picture of how pregenital this sexuality is. It's all about eating and defaecating.

MM: Then she makes the following associations, after saying that she didn't want to tell her dream because she was ashamed, she thought it was obscene: 'It is as if the supervisor were you, she is giving you the *Three Essays on Sexuality,* and she is very kind to write up an evaluation.' Then she says: 'The yard and the bench appear to be those of a house where I used to live from age four to eleven years; the maid masturbated me when I was four, she interfered with me. My brother and I also masturbated each other. We would go to my parents' bed and make a *cabana.*'

DM: This is all part of the story and it may or may not be factually true. But it's very important that the analyst shouldn't believe it and use it as evidence that she has been a masturbating child from very early on. If you used this to interpret the transference, you would be interpreting to her that she experiences everything in the transference as a seduction and that she is not responsible for her mental states. These are only the consequence of her being seduced into states of confusion. The evidence of the dreams and of her behaviour, however, is that she has a great preference for this fruit salad of confusion and begins to spark and explode any time the analyst indicates that she is responsible for her mental states.

MM: She has a third association: 'Ipanema is where I had an affair with a man, a doctor who cured me of my obsession with thinking about food (remember I already told you about this), and it was also where I had an affair with a guy who took off his condom and ejaculated inside me. He wanted to see me again, but I said that I was going to marry J, and I got angry at him.'

DM: What a reprimand! How dare you ejaculate in me when you know I'm going to marry another man. You dirty man! The man who cured her of this obsession with food is the first man who gave her his penis to suck.

MM: I don't intend to relate all this work, but there is one more detail which is extremely interesting, that is, the choice of words in the dream. For example: the Copacabana of the dream is also the *cabana* (cabin in English) of the association she made. Ipanema also has something to do with her analysis and with the psychoanalytic institution (IPA). I won't elaborate on this, because we are working along a different line.

DM: I suppose this glass of meconic fluid is really meconium, the fluid in the womb soiled with meconium.

Let me summarise. First of all, this is an important illustration of the kind of patient who welcomes confusion, because the case also demonstrates what the confusion is about. The confusion is about responsibility for mental states. The preference for masturbation and acting-out is for the purpose of creating this confusion in which other people are responsible because of their seductions. The other interesting thing about it is that this confusion, in a sense, has a very important link with the *Three Essays on Sexuality*, where Freud confuses the issue between infantile sexuality and perversity.

You can see in this material how delicate is this border-line between the polymorphism of infantile sexuality, with its preponderant pregenital eroticism, and the sado-masochism of perversity. Freud's term, polymorphously perverse, had the effect, really, of enshrining this confusion. Its consequences were a continuing confusion between pregenital and pre-oedipal, and the perpetuation of the concept of pre-oedipal in the psychoanalytic literature.

Participant: I am very curious, because the manifest content of the dreams was taken as all the dream, almost not needing interpretation. In my experience, it is very rare that a person has dreams with the infantile content so explicit. I don't usually see this. Another interesting aspect is that the series of dreams always has the person of the analyst present. What role does she have in all this?

DM: First of all, it varies from patient to patient. There are patients who dream continually about the analyst, and there are other patients with whom you have to really search the material for evidence of the transference. In either case, the so-called manifest content is not manifest in its meaning at all. You don't discover the meaning of any dream until you recognise the symbol formation that's involved. The symbol-formation involved in the dream is seldom given in the visual image only. You have to add to the visual image the language with which is described. The idea that I am just interpreting the manifest content doesn't take into account that I am continually searching for the symbol-formation and interpreting the symbols.

For instance, the dream in which the teacher has black hair and thick red lips is being seen as symbolic of the female genital as a part-object. Of course, it is true that many of the symbols that you meet in a patient's dream are perfectly obvious because they are received symbols. They are symbolic formulations that are so present in the culture that you can read them off quite directly. This is characteristic of material related to the paranoid-schizoid position. As soon as you get to the threshold of the depressive position and beyond, you run into autonomous symbol formation. These symbols certainly cannot be read off directly because they are, first of all, more condensed, more complicated, and usually involve the aesthetic level of meaning. In a word, they are more poetic. The symbols of the paranoid-schizoid position, like the symbols of children's play, are absolutely transparent. It's of interest travelling around the world that you see these symbols are very little different from culture to culture.

Participant: In the previous question, there was a second part that asked what the role of the analyst was in this type of dream formation.

DM: That sort of question brings us to the privacy of the countertransference. In a public situation, and even in a private supervision, it isn't something that a supervisor is in a position to comment on. These are matters between the therapist and her own analyst. There's always a problem in analysis of respecting people's privacy, whether it's the patient's or the analyst's.

Participant: Could the fact, for example, that she is a teacher, that she has an training in education, have any importance in this situation?

DM: I don't know. That's between her and her analyst.

Participant: I would like to ask if this explicit presentation of sexuality and masturbation by the patient couldn't be viewed as a way of hiding some other thing, as if the patient wanted to entertain the analyst, seducing her with extremely erotic material. Could there be come other thing hidden here, the depressive position of the patient, for example; couldn't she be trying to create an illusory situation of excitement, when there is something else behind it? Couldn't it be a defensive position?

DM: As I said last night, the preoccupation with the dynamic aspect of metapsychology has great limitations as a therapeutic instrument. If it's not a vicious circle, it's a benign circle in which everything is because, because, because … and is soon biting its own tail.

One thing to be said about the countertransference with patients who present very explicit erotic material, is the problem of it provoking a pornographic impact on the therapist. If you follow dreams, as I believe most people do, with visual imagination, it can be very much like looking at a pornographic film. But that isn't in itself enough to explain its having an erotic impact. I don't think you can protect yourself from the countertransference by turning your eyes away as it were. I think one has to look at the pornographic image and search it for its meaning and deal with any state of arousal it seems to generate in you.

Second seminar

Marisa Mélega: One month after the last dream I related yesterday, about Copacabana and Ipanema, the patient related another dream: *There was water in the Rio de Janeiro lodging, a lot of water. I walked in it, and there were faeces on the ground too. Should I clean it? Or was there someone else to do it? Was I to clean with a broom and a shovel, or was I to use toilet paper? A pair of lacy pink panties was highlighted. The hospital appears, as well as myself, my sister, and her dog, a poodle. Is it mine? Then it isn't hers? I lose the dog, and we start looking for it. I wake up in distress, but I wanted to keep on dreaming, wanted to remain in the water.*

Then she starts crying.

Two months later, I return to work a week before the date planned, but I had to leave again in two weeks' time. She complains that she can't control me, that I come and go whenever I like. Then she says, 'It was difficult to find time to come to analysis. It was so good that you arrived before, bringing movement and life. I stopped having insomnia.' And then she tells me two dreams. The first: *I was taking care of a baby, cleaning diapers when I saw myself with excrement in my mouth; I became distressed and couldn't remove it, I tried with a spatula.*

The second dream: *I dreamt about you telling me that you had come back sooner, that I opened my mouth and inside was blood-covered cotton wool, it looked like a tampax and menstrual blood.*

Donald Meltzer: You can see that we are in the realm of terrific zonal confusion. In a way, this represents an improvement of everything in the transference. The patient now feels the confusion between mouth and genitals. In a way this means an evolution in genitalisation and transference. The confusion is seen between mouth and genitals, as it was between saliva and faeces, menstrual blood and faeces, and this is accompanied by a feeling of losing control over the analyst because, unfortunately, this loss of control over the analyst is given a certain external reality by the changes of schedule. At the same time, the instability and insecurity is giving her more of a feeling of life, of the relationship being alive, and some improved differentiation between internal and external, which results in her sleeping better.

You have here an illustration of the difference between being confused – which the patient doesn't notice, doesn't feel as distressing – and the improved state of feeling confused, which feels terrible. This distinction is very important thing to bear in mind, that is, between being confused and feeling confused. While it represents a metapsychological improvement, the patient complains because it feels worse. Patients are likely to complain about anything that feels worse, and be puzzled that the analyst views this as an improvement. It is more or less the same sort of problem that we spoke about yesterday, in terms of the patient's concern with the painfulness of pain, and the analyst's interest in the meaning of pain, which of course the patient is likely to view as a kind of heartlessness, cruelty.

MM: Almost three months after the last dream, she says that she feels her state of anxiety is better. She tells me a dream: *I was going to volleyball practice, but I was in the bathroom smoking, hiding from the coach, who was strict. I woke up in distress.*

DM: You can be sure that hiding in the bathroom is a way to represent masturbation.

MM: The other dream: *The laundry room of my house appeared, outside the main part, and two or three men were walking on the roof. I was worried that they would break the tiles. The men and the tiles were disproportionate, with the tiles looking huge and the men tiny. Then the roof appeared as it was, but with new tiles in some places and there was a new little roof like the ones you see on mailboxes. I felt relieved.*

DM: This is a dream in which she recognises an improvement, also represented in a roughly symbolical way. The mailbox stands for the patient's mind and its capacity to receive communications; and the image of little men on the roof is a representation of having penises in the brain, and these are shrinking, which reduces the danger of them entering her mind. This is the kind of improvement provoked by the change from being confused to feeling confused. The laundry room is a representation of the cleaning process of her dirty mind, since she is a girl with an amazingly dirty mind. It is a pregenital sexuality, a pregenital Oedipus complex, which is always mixed up with faeces.

MM: Then, the following month, she describes a scene of her dancing with her husband, and her son waiting to get between them. Then her husband invites the son to dance. There are three dreams. The first: *A baby appears; he has the eyes of the man I had an affair with at a certain point during the analysis.* The second dream: *I was in bed with my uncle, my father's brother, naked, dark skin, a touch of the hand on the shoulder blade, he looks thin, like a young boy. He ejaculates on my leg and says it isn't the right place, that the job was badly done.* The third dream: *I was in bed with a man friend and there was a window with dirty iron squares. I said that the windows needed cleaning, because his wife was going to arrive.*

DM: The process of continually feeling confused happens not only in dreams, but also in the waking state. The preoccupation with penises, in a state of confusion, does not differentiate itself from the faeces, which also appeared in the dream in which she had faeces in her mouth. In the little men on the roof and in the mailbox we can recognise something dirty, which means promiscuity close to prostitution. There is the recognition that having a right place and a right person goes against promiscuous eroticism.

MM: In the following session, she brings a new dream: *I dreamt I was in X and I had to pass a plot of land opposite the house, and it was full of dead people, corpses; they seemed to be covered but they smelled, and flies were hovering around them. I didn't know how to get through it. At the end of it there was a dog with a puppy, which seemed to be dead. I had to go through it, jump over a wall, and get to the back of the plot. I managed to do it, and there was Maria* (a maid who had just retired) *with two babies on either arm; both were very small and seemed to be newborn, but they were chubby and fair-skinned. She had to hang the washing on the line, and I asked myself how she was going to do it since she had both children in her arms.*

She makes various associations. X was a place where she worked as a volunteer attending people in prison; it was also where her grandmother used to live, a big house with lots of servants, where she used to stay a lot when five or six years old. The dog was like that belonging to her grandmother. At five her nanny found her a private teacher to teach her to write and read at home. Her nanny also chose the school she was going to attend and enrolled her there. Her brother was born during this period. In that house there was a boy-servant who had been raised by her grandmother. She recalls one time sitting in the veranda of that house, and saying she wanted to be her newborn baby brother, since he was not aware his parents had gone out to the cinema, leaving them with the nanny. Then she recalled the gifts – clothes and lipstick – her father used to give her mother, as well as the gifts she used to get from him. She also recalled being beaten by her father because she had called the boy-servant a 'son of a bitch'.

DM: The important thing about this kind of material is that you can see how the analyst is identified with the servants in her childhood, with people who do the dirty work, such as taking care of babies, changing diapers, washing bedclothes. It is the kind of thing I call dependence on the 'toilet-mother', which, according to cultural differences in childhood, is shared by parents and servants. In rich families, servants often do the dirty work of bringing up children. But you can see that, in this dependence on the analyst as a servant, it is hard for the patient to trust she is capable of this hard task, since there is so much dirt.

It's interesting to notice that the task of cleaning the patient's mind as well as her bottom is implied by the tasks involved in childhood development, such accepting the birth of a sibling, learning how to read; cleaning the mind means she doesn't have to call her brother 'son of a bitch'.

MM: Three months later, she tells the following dream: *The first scene in the dream takes place on a veranda looking onto the yard of a house, a bit like the one of my childhood. My mother and I are on the veranda. This veranda is like a room, but one of the walls is missing. An external wall supports the roof. There is a pillar almost in the middle of it. Leaning against the pillar there* *is a ceramic flowerpot in which a tree was growing with a dark brown trunk, cylindrical (without any branches) and on the top, a crown which was small compared to the height of the trunk. The tree looked like a thin person, the crown was the size of an adult's head. The leaves were dark green and small. I was terrified that a monster would emerge from the flowerpot, dark and flabby; the darkness was 'black mud', like a black mollusc, also like coagulated menstrual blood.*

I could not figure how my mother could be so calm; either she did not understand my fear or she treated it as a childish folly. Suddenly an animal sprang from inside the flower pot, it gave a graceful leap. It was black, very hairy, like a cat but with a squarer body and a fuller face. It did not touch the ground but its face went on fire and it disappeared into thin air.

Then I was inside the house, separated from the veranda but a slatted door like the wardrobe doors in my present house. The door had an opening like a window. My aunt whom I like a lot and who lives in São Paulo was with me. I look out at the veranda, my left hand resting on the window, and see an animal with a body like that of a giraffe, and a round face like that of a cat or a lioness. Its coat was short-haired and piebald, white with grey patches. It began to approach me as I looked at it, and my left hand and forearm began to take on the same skin as the animal. I became very frightened, I seemed to be turning into the animal. I moved away from the door feeling distressed. My aunt went up to the opening in the window, called the animal, patted it, and told me I needn't be afraid, that it was a pet animal and wouldn't do me any harm.

She said this second animal reminded her of a dog they had in the house of her childhood, which was large and very fierce, a Dalmatian or a setter; the animal's skin looked like that of the dog.

DM: Listening to these dreams of the patient's, which she is able to recall in detail, is like seeing a child drawing. You see the exact representation of the continuous change in form, in meaning, of a person into an animal, from one body zone to another. And also the distinction between internal and external, represented by the veranda, the way the entrance to the house can appear at any moment. All this is exactly the way children draw, and it expresses the child's problem of being in a state of confusion owing to depending on adults in order to interpret the meaning of the world. It's a total dependence, that is, she depends on an adult to tell her she doesn't have to fear anything.

With this patient, the great frightening confusion is between faeces and penis. This implies a preoccupation with defaecation. The differentiation between vagina and rectum is so incomplete that it is represented only by a wall, which she can easily jump over. The differentiation between good and docile animals and wild and dangerous ones (as qualities of the penis) is also a reference to the flabby penis and the erect one. And jumping over is also a representation of ejaculation. You have the impression of a child who did not only masturbate, but was also exposed to primary scenes.

But this kind of dependence on a mother-servant to clean all the dirt – including the dirt of the mind – and to make the differentiation between safe and dangerous, and eventually between beautiful and ugly, is a very childish process. She is a very unsophisticated patient. The material is almost the same as that in a room where a five or six year-old child plays, drawing rough shapeless pictures, with scribbling standing for anxieties, where things suddenly burst into flames. 'What colour is that? It's fire.' Sexual excitement is represented by the danger of fire.

Participant: What factors can contribute to a person becoming so stuck in the pre-oedipal phase, with so many geographical confusions?

DM: I do not agree it is pre-oedipal, but pregenital. The factor that holds a child within this pregenital phase usually has its origin in sphincter control, and the factor perpetuating such confusion is secret masturbation. Secret masturbation counts on the parents' collusion, often represented by their satisfaction when children are not making any trouble, any noise. I like to describe this kind of parental collusion through a joke: 'What are you doing, children?' asks their mother when children are quiet upstairs. 'We're fucking, mother.' And mother answers: 'Good children. Don't quarrel.' The essence of parental collusion is that everything is valid so long there is peace and quiet.

Participant: You are giving great structural importance to the external factor. Do you really think so?

DM: Emphasising does not mean treating bits of the story as if they were facts. I prefer imaginative constructions which can often be told as jokes, but that apprehend the truth of the family's situation in a stereotyped way. We can recognise the importance of reinforcement by the environment, without considering it causal or explanatory. The crucial point is the secretiveness of the child. Parental control can be either benevolent or persecutory. It is largely the child's perception that determines if it is benevolent or persecutory. Only parents know what is inside themselves. And parents can exert a form of watchfulness that children can feel to be persecutory: such as, smelling a small child's hands to check if he or she was masturbating, or inspecting the sheets of an adolescent boy to check if he has been ejaculating, will probably be regarded as persecutory. There is a malicious quality to this kind of interest – looking for dirt. When you see signs of masturbation beware that your tone of voice does not sound like that of the KGB: 'Aha, you were masturbating.' Your tone should indicate you know your children masturbate, and you don't mind that, but you do mind the meaning of masturbation and the secretive way it is done.

I know that analysts all over the world find it difficult to talk to their patients about masturbation. They expect their patients to talk about it, but it is not necessarily the case. You can describe the signs of childish sexuality and the evidence that it is something pregenital. We rarely find such a childish patient as this one. Most of our patients are more sophisticated than this girl, but the problems she shows are frequent.

Participant: I would like Dr Meltzer to help me to analyse something that has intrigued me: the huge quantity of dreams brought by this patient sometimes gives the feeling of not only invasion, but even of a certain disinterest, for the analyst's attention is demanded minutely in a very tiring way. I would like to know why this patient presents everything in such a detailed way. This makes me think of a show-off, voyeuristic relationship; I wonder if this girl is not asking for a mother to simply accept this pregenital life, to collude with it, perhaps not leaving much room for understanding, since the patient in a sense anaesthetises the analyst.

DM: What you are pointing out demands a very careful discrimination between the childish patient who still suffers from zonal and geographical confusion (and the inevitable confusion between good and bad) and the sadomasochistic patient who intends to dirty the analyst, to excite and corrupt her. This is one of the reasons why I emphasise this patient's childishness. In this sense, her material is very innocent; it is as if she had diarrhoea: it is necessary to wash her dirty diapers all the time. And it is not only one intestinal movement a day, but twenty. Just as mothers feel they are going to spend the rest of their lives washing diapers, this is naturally boring, tedious, but it does not make you feel dirty, as a sadomasochist does. Thus, I think this is an important differentiation in terms of the countertransference. You may feel the material to be disagreeable, but it does not make you feel attacked.

MM: I would like to make something clear: I am presenting dreams from a five-year analysis, in order to illustrate this patient's childish sexuality. Thus, my presentation may seem rather disproportionate.

DM: It is even worse owing to such a long time span. When collecting this kind of material from a patient you may think: 'My God, this is going to go on for five years!' But such is a mother's life. When you have a patient like this, you have a baby with diarrhoea, and it seems to go on forever.

Participant: I was impressed: in one of the dreams, the patient places the laundry room separate from the house. This brought to mind Dr Meltzer saying that analytical work aims to provide new tools which can eventually enrich the internal object. Can this laundry room, which the patient acknowledges to be useful and found outside the house, as a representation of the 'toilet-breast', be one such tool, a tool for discriminating that what she is thinking is dirty and must be cleaned? Why was the laundry room no longer mistaken with the general structure of the house?

DM: When you talk about discrimination and the instruments of discrimination, you are using the language of psychoanalytical theory, because what happens in the patient is a matter of personality structure, reinforced by the family structure and the culture the child belongs to. For example, in patients growing up in South Africa the representation of the small huts where servants live at the back of gardens is not only the place where dirty work is done, but also the place of sexuality, and this emphasises the splitting process. It is hard to overcome this and join these split objects, and it is a prerequisite for the combined object. But it is a matter of reinforcement, not one of cause and effect. In the case of South Africa, the servants' house is not only the place for dirty work and sexuality, but it is also a place for all tenderness. And a connection involving tenderness with the servants may reinforce the tendency to treat parents as distant figures. You certainly have to take into consideration the role of environment in the development of children, but its meaning depends on the child's willingness and temperament, as well as on the development of secrecy.

Participant: Could you please speak further about the development of secrecy?

DM: There are two kinds of secrecy: the secrecy of isolation, and the secrecy of collusion. The secrecy of isolation is what you see in only children or in children with a considerable age difference between siblings; it is accompanied by so much loneliness that analytical investigation is welcome. The secrecy of collusion, which characteristically occurs in identical twins or, to a lesser degree, with siblings nearly the same age, is usually built in a sadomasochist way. And as with all sadomasochists, it is very resistant to analytical investigation. This differentiation is important, for it warns us about the difficulties and slowness of analytical work, which depends on the patient's cooperation and also on the mobility of the patient's structural organisation. The analyst has little influence over mobility of imagination, and has to tolerate the patient's different values.

The most important value, love of truth, does not usually manifest itself at the beginning of an analysis, and the analyst needs to accept that the patient does not realise that truth and beauty are synonymous. This demands a certain degree of tolerance.

Participant: Do you think that in cases where the secrecy is of isolation, the analytical job is easier, since a sadomasochistic element is absent?

DM: I meant that what makes analysis welcome is the fact that the secrecy of isolation is extremely lonely. With this kind of patient, the emphasis in the analytical work falls upon maintaining an intimate contact. One of the factors making this easier is the analyst's attitude towards guilt. In my view, guilt does not facilitate development; guilt demands and expects punishment and it is important that the analyst does not reinforce guilt, but help it to change into repentance. Repentance acknowledges that nothing can be done about it; while guilt demands punishment, as if punishment were a form of reparation. It is interesting to notice that in the *Divine Comedy*, Dante always shows people in hell running to meet their punishment; it is true. Patients run after punishment, and if you reinforce this, before you realise it you are in a confessional situation, which does not lead in the direction of development.

Participant: Is this related to the question of the concept of forgiveness you referred to in *Dream Life*?

DM: Yes, it is. Forgiveness is certainly a central concept in psychoanalysis, and it should not be confused with Christian forgiveness, in which submission to punishment results in reward. The great biblical example is the story of Job, which is about God's shocking indifference when he submits Job to a series of bereavements in order to exhibit his power to Satan. There is a similar story about Hitler during the war showing off to journalists the dedication of his soldiers, by ordering them to jump off a plane with no parachutes. When a soldier was about to jump off, a journalist asked him: 'Why are you doing it? Why are you about to sacrifice your own life for this man?' And the soldier answered: 'Do you call this a life?'

Participant: Could you say more about the philosophical characteristics of forgiveness, from the viewpoint you have mentioned?

DM: We could mention the example of a Jewish boy forgiving the Nazis. It needs only a little imagination for the boy to tell himself – and understand – that, had he been a German boy, he would have saluted Hitler. The basis of forgiveness is the realisation that, were it not for the benevolence of my objects, I would also be a villain.

Third seminar

After these two seminars, I collected new clinical material about Brigitte to present to Dr Meltzer in some group supervisions in Oxford the following year.

Marisa Mélega: Since our last supervision in São Paulo, Brigitte had a second baby, and there has been a fifteen-month break in the analysis. I would like to recount some sessions since we resumed.

In one of these sessions, the patient enters and asks to give me the number of her mobile phone; she hands me a piece of paper which I take and place it in my address book. Her attitude indicates that she thinks I may need her and not be able to find her, which I take as a reversal of her state of dependence on me. In the previous session it had emerged for the first time that she saw herself as a daughter who was no trouble to her parents but on the contrary had helped them with their difficulties.

I now ask her if she minds her material being discussed in supervision with you, and she says she doesn't mind if it helps me. I make it clear it is for purposes of general scientific interest, and particularly of interest to both of us, within the context of her analysis.

Donald Meltzer: Both of us meaning you and she, or you and me?

MM: Me and the patient. She told me the dream that she had had the night before: *The analyst was lying with the patient, and at a certain point moved over to a second couch that made an L-shape in relation to the first. The analyst was wearing a dark-coloured flowery dress, and she made some movements over the top of her clothes, masturbating. The patient asked herself why the analyst was doing this, and thought she was upset because she had gone away.*

DM: Where these two divans connected? At the head, or at the feet?

MM: At the head, a continuation of the armchair.

DM: They are probably connected by the head of the two couches.

MM: She told me that she had never masturbated, from what she could remember, and that she began to date very early, at the age of twelve. And at once she remembers a dream she had had some days before, when recommencing analysis (she does not live in São Paulo and had to seek out the address of my new consulting room).

DM: Is it a new address from the one where she previously had analysis?

MM: Yes. In the dream *she had her hair dyed red, but not all of it. There was a gold strand, and she felt she was blonde, like me.*

DM: What colour hair does she have?

MM: Black. She comments that she is pleased to be back in analysis. She continues with her dream: *Now I get up from the couch where I was lying with you, and lie down on the L-shaped couch.* She bursts into tears, saying that she had been the one to leave.

DM: In the dream?

MM: No, out of the dream, in the session.

DM: In the dream, the patient just gets up from the couch where Marisa was lying with her, and moves over to the other couch, which is L-shaped. And then the patient bursts into tears, and says it was she who had left fifteen months ago.

MM: In the dream, she said I was very upset and masturbating, but in fact, when telling me this dream, she burst into tears, saying that she had been the one to leave.

DM: She had gone away, and masturbated, and cried, and so on.

MM: Yes. This change in state of mind is a former characteristic of this patient's. Years ago, she mixed sighs into her narrative. There was evidence of being short of breath, characteristic of greater anxiety, until she broke into convulsive sobs.

DM: This was characteristic?

MM: I believe that with her it is characteristic of episodes that have to do with an internal change from unconscious to conscious thinking. In this session, before she describes her dreams, she suddenly remembers and cries: 'Ah! That alarmed me, when my mother told me she had remarried.' I asked her how she felt about her mother's marriage. She said she was jealous, and started to go home less often, although her mother had helped her after the birth of the new baby. She does not like anyone else to touch the baby, only herself and her mother because her mother knows how she likes the baby to be looked after.

DM: She is terrifically identified with this baby, who has two mothers – a mother and a grandmother – and now, she has come back to analysis in order to have two mothers herself. But she is alarmed with the thought that in the fifteenth months she was away, maybe you have remarried as well. When she says she is jealous, it's not clear what she is jealous about, or if she is jealous or envious.

MM: Jealous because now the mother does not have time for her.

DM: She's really jealous of the new husband taking up her mother's time.

Participant: Marisa, does she know that you are divorced?

MM: No, I think she doesn't.

DM: She doesn't know. And she certainly doesn't know about your new husband. Nor do we.

MM: I don't have one. She's coming twice a week until we can find a schedule. This is the last session before the Christmas break. She says there are too many things to organise. I tell her the date when we start again, on a Monday, at the same time, and ask if she will still be on holiday; she says she will, and has all the children's things to think of …

DM: How many children does she have?

MM: Two. Two sons. She tells me two dreams from the night before: *I was going to the apartment in São Paulo with the cleaning woman. They had painted it pink. It was depressing, paint coming off, peeling, and tiles below. I thought, why have they painted it like this? It gives an impression of decadence.*

She associated it with a surprise visit she had made to her husband in his apartment in São Paulo, because she had suspicions he had a mistress. She described how she had gone through everything, and then he had arrived, and she had told him of her suspicions. I associated the colour pink and poor condition of the upper floor with the building where the consulting room is, and the bathroom in the waiting room which had undergone repair work, and had now been plastered and painted. The patient had not thought of this, but she believes this connection is possible. She associates it with her father's bad condition when he left home.

The second dream: *They had broken into her building by forcing the glass windows above the stairs leading up to her apartment* (she explains that these are high windows, and that they are difficult to clean), *and she was afraid of being alone with her children, but somebody had assured her that there would be no danger.*

Her husband works in São Paulo; they live in another city.

DM: How far from São Paulo?

MM: It's about a hundred miles, about two hours by car.

DM: They have a flat in São Paulo that was originally his?

MM: They bought a flat when her husband was obliged to come to work in São Paulo because there was no work for him in the city where they live.

DM: She suspected that he had a mistress in this flat, which is painted pink. In fact, is it painted pink?

MM: No, it isn't. I tell her, she was really experiencing the return to analysis as an assault, and the wish to return to analysis she felt as being mine, not hers: I am forcing her to learn about depressing things. She agrees, and says she feels she is drawing closer to her husband, less defensive and more able to converse about things, rather than 'brooding on her anger'. Also she had been going to remind the maid to clean the bathroom when she came the next time, then thought, why not tell her now? and she did.

I remark that I think she is calling attention to the difference between free association where things are meaningfully connected, and the type of organisation that tries to keep meanings separate from each other. What do you think about this?

DM: It's a little intellectual.

MM: The patient says the idea distresses her; she thinks it has to do with her defences. But organising things in their right place makes her feel more at ease.

DM: The material about her relationship with her husband and how it's connected to the analysis is quite clear. She has a very strong maternal transference to you, but a very erotic one. When she feels broken into, she's not sure if it is her husband breaking into her, when they have sexual intercourse, or you breaking into her when she has analysis with you. In either, she's feeling a bit frightened and a bit violated by either you, or her husband, or both of you. Of course, 'both of you' means either that she suspects that you are remarried, as in the news about the mother, or that perhaps you are the husband's mistress, and that in the fifteen months when she didn't come to analysis, he substituted himself into her place as your lover. She is full of suspicions really.

MM: And also referring to the subject of this supervision, I think.

DM: The whole thing is that she is feeling exploited by all of you.

Fourth seminar

Marisa Mélega: She missed the first session. An unforeseen event. She said she thought she didn't want to come, because she was tired. But then she felt guilty. She felt she was plain.

Participant: She has two sessions on the same day?

MM: Yes. The other two days, one session each.

Donald Meltzer: On Monday she has two sessions? What is the time difference between the sessions?

MM: Three hours.

DM: Is she plain or is she good-looking?

MM: She is good-looking. She brings a dream: *You* (the analyst) *were plainer, slightly shorter than me. I lay down, and you kept walking around the room, and stopped in front of me. You were talking, gesticulating* (she starts to cry) *and all of a sudden, it was like a psychiatric hospital. There were one million people to rescue,* *and two of us …* (she continues to cry). *When we got close there was a foetus or a small child, and we said mind the head, we have to be careful.*

DM: 'We' is you and she?

MM: Yes.

She couldn't get to the next session, as there was a problem on the motorway, and she phoned from her mobile, so I suggested an extra session the next day. When she arrived she thanked me, and I said it was in order to maintain the analytic work. She said, 'I'm not a lady', and I found this strange; I said she felt a certain expectation on my part.

DM: Yes, she prefers to be treated like the maid, and told: 'Clean the bathroom.' She asks: 'Well, why didn't I tell the maid to clean the bathroom now – why do I have to wait until the next cleaning day?' And you tell her: 'Oh, you couldn't come today. Come on Tuesday, and then you can clean the bathroom on Tuesday.'

MM: I understood that offering a replacement session would be regarded as a seduction. Is that right?

DM: Doing it as if you were being kind to her is felt as a piece of hypocrisy, when you are really giving orders to the maid. She is much more comfortable being treated as your maid, because you are the lady, and she is the maid, and if there is any seduction here, it's you who does it: the lady seduces the maid, the maid doesn't seduce the lady.

MM: Is it about the difficulty in accepting and receiving – does she feel indebted? Does the analyst have secondary intentions?

DM: She would be much happier for you to be indebted to her for her hard work in cleaning up *your* dirty bathroom than for her to be indebted to you because you clean up *her* dirty bathroom, as the baby.

MM: She was filled with worries over the weekend. At the next session she expressed concern over her son who was starting a new class at school, and whether he was going to have problems. She has been thinking about the maid who did not do exactly what she wanted, and acknowledges she is a good maid after all.

DM: Yes, she lives in projective identification inside you, but very useful as your maid, cleaning your toilet, not you as her mother cleaning her bottom. She as your maid cleaning your toilet, because you mess it up with your masturbation. You a masturbating mother, and she is a good little maid girl who cleans up the bathroom.

MM: In the next session on the same day, as she had asked for this, I make a summary in response to her reflections on previous sessions. Then she remembers a dream: *In Rio de Janeiro, I had no place to live, and I saw two houses. I went inside them, and they were not separate. You could go from one to the other, and there were swimming pools. I think, it is a good thing I can sleep here.*

DM: Back in the bed with you, inside, going freely to different compartments, from the rectum to the vagina, to the breast, swimming pools. Lovely being inside you, not at all claustrophobic.

MM: This is a dream from the next session: *My husband was cheating on me, seated with his legs apart, and a girl between his legs, dressed, but with a bare breast, wearing only the bottom of a minute bikini. I say to my mother that I think I'm going to ask for a separation.*

DM: If you are going to do things like that with husband-daddy, I'm not going to stay inside you and be your maid, and you'll be sorry, you'll be crying.

MM: The patient says: 'I wake up and wonder whether I have to get a separation from him or not.'

DM: She suspects that you have been his mistress during the fifteen months that she was away, and being your maid is really not such a nice thing because when she is inside you, she has to realise that her husband comes to visit you and has intercourse with you, and so on.

MM: Her next dream: *I am in the garden of my house with you, and the gate is in three parts that tilt outwards to open. You show me that the gate is in the middle of the garden, and go away. And then I see that it is so, that every time it opens, it drags on the ground, and that it is in fact rotten, it looks like swings in a* *children's playground. And I wonder what I am supposed to do with this piece of junk, I am filled with worry.*

As she proceeds with the description, she becomes emotional.

DM: There is a gate between the rectum and the vagina, but as it swings, it brings with it some of the faeces from the rectum and makes a mess, and this is what she, as a maid, has to clean up all the time, the mess from the rectum.

MM: We have, for some weeks, been following up these movements where there is a barrier between her and another, like the two houses that in face have no dividing walls. In this session, she recalled the euphoria of being able to pass from one environment to another, jumping up in the air like the the tilting gate that merged with the swing.

DM: She is getting more claustrophobic.

MM: We have been working considering the real limits of her personality, as against the boundaries that she fantasises, in which she feels she must care for all who belong to her scenario in order to feel that things will be fine. She then feels burdened and intolerant with those who have faults.

DM: She's getting fed up with being your maid and living in your rectum.

MM: After the weekend, she says she had a difficult weekend, but felt better. I say she can use her analysis to deal with her experiences. (The previous week, she said she used excitement and making love in to order to feel alive.) We then talked about her fear of relying on others, on the one hand, and on the other, her insecurity about being independent. The next session she delivers a narrative that could be summed up as: 'If I feel I can use my analysis, then I am also afraid of not knowing what to do when I don't have it.'

I think the patient is making progress in the distinction between self and object. She can now accept the existence of the other.

DM: I'm not sure. I mean, it's possible that she is being forced out of projective identification by the claustrophobia, but the claustrophobia has this structure: that her husband keeps appearing in your vagina, while she is cleaning up the toilet and the rectum. This makes life very difficult, and she thinks she wants to have a separation from this man or from the situation, from the analyst. The whole thing is getting unbearable, really.

MM: From this period on, she starts missing sessions.

Next time, she comes in a state of distress, having scolded her son for overloading his dinner plate and filling his mouth. 'I went to fetch a mirror so he could see himself.' Then she starts to cry.

DM: Projective identification with the son and defence against separation, and so on.

MM: I say she feels we have both failed in the analysis. The patient said she just repeats everything: 'I blame my parents. They were a mess.'

The session after this she feels better and does not just repeat everything. She dreamed about the analyst. What do you think of the fact that this woman is always dreaming about the analyst?

DM: She has a strong erotic homosexual transference to you, as your maid; and then, being exposed to your sexuality with men, as the nursemaid. This behaviour with her son is really her jealousy of the new baby – your new baby, her new baby. Is she breastfeeding the baby?

MM: She did breastfeed. Now the baby is one year old.

DM: And she really is jealous of this baby at the breast and sees him as your baby at your breast, and is quite cruel, holds the mirror up to him, and says: 'See what a mess you are, you greedy little baby.'

MM: This is the dream: *You* (the analyst) *were wearing a blue dress, talking, and you understood about kidneys and oriental medicine. I was curious to learn more about you. Your boyfriend was in a loose, big blue shirt. I was the one who was too short. I was trying to flirt with him, since I felt attracted by him.*

DM: The analyst's boyfriend, who is also her husband.

MM: And then in the dream *she was in a swimming pool in a closed place: 'me with you, in and out.'* Then, she started to cry. She does not know why.

DM: She's having a sexual relationship with you.

Participant: This 'in and out' gives a kind of movement.

DM: She is having a sexual relationship with you in which sucking at your breast is not distinguished from licking your clitoris or something of that sort. This, too, gets confused with being the boyfriend's penis going in and out of you, and so on. The whole thing is very confused at a zonal level. It may be that she is out because she was feeling very claustrophobic, and she may be now, temporarily, out of the claustrum. 'And you understood about kidneys.'

MM: In reality she has a normal life.

DM: But she has a rich fantasy life and she is a masturbator, and the transference is a very erotic infantile transference, full of confusion. 'You know about kidneys, oriental medicine. I was curious to know more about you.' I don't know what this kidneys and oriental medicine is about.

MM: The bottom.

DM: It's probably the bottom.

MM: The emotion of feeling the analyst looking after her. She was ill. She felt ill this weekend. She felt crazy.

DM: So, instead of *being* confused, she is beginning to *feel* confused, and feeling much crazier.

MM: It's progress.

DM: Yes.

MM: Soon after this she comes with the following dream: *There is a large table with some men in large robes, togas, kaftans, and she does a striptease and puts her breast up against the table to excite them, and between her breasts is a baby trying to make itself noticed.* (She cries.)

DM: There you get the picture that breastfeeding the baby does really excites her sexually because she imagines your boyfriend, your husband, watching her and getting excited.

MM: She woke up feeling so awful that she thought she would call me for an extra session.

DM: There's the baby in the middle of the night, who's got to wake mummy: 'Bring the breast, bring the breast.'

MM: The struggle has been against dependence, relying on others. Later she told a second dream: *I was on my way to São Paulo with the driver, and he is excited about me, and I think what should I do. I don't want him. I want my husband.*

DM: That's daddy carrying her to be fed at the breast by mother, and feeling that he is very excited about this little girl of his. Really, he used to be her husband when he was inside mummy. Now he is just the driver who carries her to the mummy. She wants a husband. She liked it when she was inside mummy and he was the husband. Now she misses it, although it makes her feel a bit crazy really.

MM: The next session comes just before a holiday. At one moment, during the session, she says that on her way back home, she drifted off to sleep in the car, and *she saw the image of a woman lying down with her legs on the ground and she was close to her vagina.*

DM: Is she sucking at the breast, or is she looking at your clitoris?

MM: She awoke feeling more alive. She left the session much relieved following her tense week. She says that now she is better. She doesn't believe she has an insoluble problem with her husband. I try to help her see that outside the sessions she must continue thinking about what has happened to her during the analytic contact; it is very important to be aware of this so that there is no acting out. She understands this. This is not my usual way of interpretation.

DM: She is an acting-out patient, and it is very important to warn her against acting-out. With a dream like this, it means that every time the baby sucks her breast, she's going to have fantasies of sucking your vagina and will scold her little boy for filling his mouth and so on. It's all acting-out, so it's necessary to warn her against a tendency to act out.

MM: We are also working on her mental functioning, how she attempts to join up and control parts of her mind and personality. Her need to tidy up comes from the need to be continually tidying her inner chaos, or the parts of herself felt as confused, out of place.

DM: That is, your maid in your rectum, cleaning up the toilet.

MM: And with a need to keep busy, committed to bodily sensations rather than forming thoughts – different from being articulated, connected.

DM: Again, it's necessary to show her these things, I think.

MM: The other day she was full of her plans to remodel her house and spoke of her wish, that she cannot yet carry out, to build a large room to dance in.

DM: *To dance*. She's an action girl, and it's necessary to tell her continually about the contrast between thinking and acting because her impulse is always to act, to put it into action immediately, because she has difficulty getting her thoughts clear. She thinks that if she thinks, she just gets more confused. Without you to do her thinking for her, she finds herself confused, so she starts dancing. She's a good girl really. Is her husband a nice fellow?

MM: I don't know. He seems to be very intelligent. He's an engineer, graduated from the ITA, which is a top place for training engineers.

I would like to say something about Brigitte's movements. All through the first year of analysis, she would speak and speak and seem to be moving towards some insight, then burst into tears and another subject would emerge. It was as if she and I were walking along a path with a purpose, then suddenly we came upon a new scene where new infantile material would emerge.

DM: Of course, it happens in dreams very frequently. Suddenly, the ambience of the dream changes. It is a way of representing and experiencing a sudden change of mental state. I think it usually has to do with falling into projective identification because what you see in dreams is that they enter into a huge hall, or suddenly find themselves in the basement of a big hotel, or things of this sort.

Participant: Would this be the Claustrum, Dr Meltzer?

DM: The way it happens, I think, in fact, is that a kind of gentle masturbatory or gentle sexual play is going one, and then suddenly there is an orgasm. It's like a patient of mine who was playing with her toes, and then suddenly there was an orgasm, and the room began to rise, and she saw the dome, and so on. It is the masturbatory orgasm that brings tremendous changes in the state of mind. Sometimes, it explodes the patient out of projective identification, and they get terrifically depressed. Sometimes, it sucks them into projective identification, and they get horrifically confused, but it is a geographical change.

Participant: Could we see the dreams as a kind of twilight zone between a projective identification dream world and, let's say, a symbolic world?

DM: I would be more inclined to see the experiences in the outside world as a kind of twilight world, where meaning is not clear, though things appear very factual, and that it is in dreams that the meaning of things becomes suddenly clear. This is the reason patients who are so committed to life in the outside world don't dream, and don't want to dream, and when they start to dream, they feel invaded by their dreams, which are so full of meaning and so full of emotion. They much prefer to live in the outside world where it is business as usual. You know what the price of things is, and you know how much money you have in your pocket.

The personality is very complicated really. I used to think that projective identification produced the 'as if' personality, but I think that it's much more complicated than this. It corresponds to what Winnicott calls the 'false self', and comes from projective identification. But the question is, 'Which is the true self, and which is the false self?' I think he gets it wrong actually.

So it is not a twilight zone. It's a zone of meaning and emotion, and, of course, the place where confusion becomes apparent. In the outside world, everything is (except at times of war and so on) orderly and organised. That orderly world is greatly preferred to the world of turbulent emotion, and thought, and confusion.

Participant: Which is also the world of creativity you spoke about yesterday with Milton.

DM: It is the world of *potential* creativity. There are patients whose dream life is very rich in the sense of being very varied and abundant, and so on, without there being anything creative about it because there is relatively little symbolism. It's mostly taken from the outside world and just made into an internal world drama. This is not creative. This is where dreams and daydreams are almost the same thing and come close to Freud's formulation of the function of the dream as wish fulfilment. But the creative dreams are ones where extraordinary symbol-formation takes place, and this takes place with terrific condensation.

The meaning of such dreams jumps out as an aesthetic object. My patient dreamt about the dome of the Duomo in Florence.

Participant: There is a Brazilian writer, Jorge Amado, who says that when he has some difficulty in his writing, he usually finds the way out of this difficulty through a dream.

DM: There is no doubt that our finest thinking takes place in our dreams. This is why the analysis of patients' dreams is so endlessly fascinating, because it is in their dreams that they are at their most imaginative.

Participant: Could you make a distinction between Freud's wish fulfilment, and this idea that you defend in your book *Dream Life*?

DM: The wish fulfilment of Freud does apply to those dreams which have a very simple childish structure like children's daydreams. The fact that they are sleep dreams hardly differentiates them from daydreams because there is very little dream work.

This patient has relatively little dream work in her dreams. They are anecdotal, and you can hardly tell the difference. You have to ask, is this a dream or is this something that happened yesterday? You wouldn't be sure because there is very little condensation. The dream about being your maid, for instance, doesn't involve a lot of symbol-formation. It's simply a reversal of the mother–baby relationship, the baby who is masturbating the mother, sucking the nipple.

MM: Different from your patient's dream.

DM: But of course, a lot of her dreams are very anecdotal also.

MM: Don't you think that condensation would be a kind of hallmark for creative dreaming?

DM: Certainly! Condensation is a constant factor in the most interesting dreams, the ones in which the symbol-formation is so rich you can peel them like an onion. This is the mysterious thing about symbols, the richness of their condensation. A good dream can be analysed for weeks. You keep getting associations that light up different parts of the dream. The dream I was speaking about with the Siena–Florence axis was really enlightening to the patient: the picture of Siena alternating with that of Florence.

Participant: This makes a kind of interface?

DM: I reminded her of the Berlin–Rome axis, which was really the interface between the dictatorships and the allies, and it was a line that gave meaning to this war. And this line, from Siena to Florence, in my consulting room, gave meaning to her. It's very similar to what Bion speaks about, the membrane between conscious and unconscious. This elaboration through alpha function forms a kind of membrane, on one side of which are conscious experiences, and on the other, symbols and unconscious experience.

MM: You talked about the condensation of the dream. What about the condensation in poetry?

DM: The condensation in really wonderful poetry has so many layers. The imagery is partly pictorial, partly historical, and partly linguistic. And it is all woven together in good poetry. I am a Keats addict.

(Here Meltzer reads out Keats' 'Ode to Psyche'.)

This poem is an absolute miracle really. It is visual, tactile, olfactory, historical, everything woven together 'with branched thoughts'.

Participant: Did Dr Bion borrow from him the concept of negative capability?

DM: From a letter to his brother.

Participant: My father was a poet, and he used to punish us by making us learn poetry by heart.

DM: That's lovely. What a lovely punishment.

Participant: Instead of hating the poets, I learned how to love them. When I was in analysis with Dr Bion, some poetry came to my mind, and I tried to translate it to him, and from the beginning, he said to me, 'Don't translate. Tell me in Portuguese. Then, if you want to, we can translate it.'

DM: Let me hear the music first.

Participant: That's right. Then I tried to translate as best as I could.

DM: It's impossible to translate.

MM: But Shakespeare has been translated.

DM: Yes, but you cannot translate good poetry. It's so dense, so interwoven, and the literal translation of the words doesn't catch the meaning at all really because it is full of the idiosyncratic meaning of the words. You can't get this out of the dictionary. It's not there. So, even the *Oxford English Dictionary* doesn't give definitions. It gives quotations of how the word is used, starting from the early years, and going up to the present. It makes very interesting reading.

Coming back to Brigitte. She's an interesting girl. She's a nice patient, very turbulent and passionate, but the erotic transference is terrific. When a patient gets into an erotic transference, they dream about the analyst night after night after night, as a child dreams about mummy and daddy.

MM: I think I didn't catch this very well.

DM: When the erotic transference is really homosexual, it's rather hard to describe to the patient. So, when you get it in the dreams, you have to just take it literally.

Participant: The dream about the couch, where the couch is connected in the L-shape.

DM: I was thinking about the one that implies the confusion between licking the nipple and licking the clitoris. [*reads*] '*You were wearing a blue dress, talking, and you understood about kidneys and oriental medicine. I was curious to learn more about you. The analyst's boyfriend was in a loose, big blue shirt. I was the one who was too short. I was trying to flirt with him, since I felt attracted by him.*' And then it sort of slips into projective identification with the analyst's boyfriend in the blue shirt. She is flirting with him, and then there's the swimming pool, and I'm with you in and out. She's a very interesting girl.

MM: This patient's parents married very young, and the mother was pregnant.

DM: They married because she was pregnant.

MM: She was born very premature, after seven months. She was very thin, very small, very difficult to feed, and there is some of this material in the last part of the presentation.

I will describe a recent session. The patient says she did not find coming into São Paulo today difficult as she had a chauffeur and could study in the car.

She tells me a dream from the night before: *I was getting home, and I could see that the house was being remodelled.* (She had mentioned remodelling the house to allow for a hall for dancing on top of the garage.) *There was no longer a flower box over the gate, a tilted gate, and I was about to go through the door, but there was no door. I pushed it, but the lower part was loose, and a dog came in. I was afraid and decided to face the dog. I held onto the dog, and together we fell to the floor in a hug. He had an enormous brown mane. I cried for help and he growled so I decided to keep quiet, and he kept quiet too, with his muzzle in my neck. I thought if I kept still, he would too. I thought of going off to sleep. I imagined a fluffy, toy dog and myself as a child hugging it and falling asleep.*

DM: This is a beautiful example of a little girl slipping into projective identification and welcoming daddy's penis coming into mummy's vagina, quite frightened of this big penis, felt to be a rather primitive animal that could savage you, but all right if you are quiet. The little girl will eventually think, 'here comes the fluffy dog', and she will kiss it, and hug it, and suck it.

MM: It seems to me that, on one level, the dream alludes to her feelings about the beginning of the approaching holidays, with the removal of the breast, gardener, nipple, door-knob analyst that then allows the entrance from below of a penis-dog to which she is attached and feels is somewhat familiar.

DM: Yes, that's a good interpretation.

MM: In yesterday's session, in tears, she became gradually aware of the analytical separation and realised how resentful she is that though she was born small and premature, her parents still continued with dancing and social activities. It seems that they manage to go ahead somehow, while she always worries about leaving everything planned and organised.

DM: You are the parents who just go off on holiday, and she has to change her own nappies and so on.

MM: And I believe that she thinks that she can avoid frustration for her children in being so very careful, but it's not possible. It is interesting to connect this with her opening statement that she did not find it so very difficult to come here today.

The next session, she tells me she feels better (this is after a week of absence due to health problems, her own and her children's). She had been afraid of 'going round the bend', going crazy. I remark that this is an old fear of hers, but now conditions are different; analysis can help her emerge from it.

She remembers a dream she had the night before: *I was living with her to show her how to make things easier. We were cooking in my kitchen for a party, preparing things and exchanging recipes. The analyst said it would be easier to buy the white sauce ready-made. Every now and then, one of us would leave, and the other would take over. On one occasion, when she was going out, she pressed the button of the lift and noticed that it was also a refrigerator.*

At this point she interrupted her narrative, convulsed in tears.

DM: You see the interplay between masturbation and sexual intercourse. Her analyst-mother is showing her the way. You don't make this white sauce yourself: you get it ready-made from your husband. And this button of mine is not your clitoris, it's my nipple. You don't have an orgasm by pressing the button of my breast. It's not the button between my legs. You are educating through differentiations, to cure her confusion, in this case, of zones. Whereas the previous dream was all about inside and outside, this is about zones, and how to get the semen. You order it ready-made from the testicles. You don't make it yourself with your finger.

She gets the message.

MM: She continues with the dream: *It was very well-equipped. This made me feel happy. At times during the dream, I felt anxious when you were teaching me like a mother what I should do to make things easier, and I tried to learn, but I was afraid I would not.*

I believe that dream is an allusion to what she will feel when she goes off on holiday. Transport, lift, part-object, penis combined with refrigerator, partially provides her with a feeding support. After five years, she is able to recognise anxieties about separation and how much she is in need of analysis.

DM: She is afraid she won't learn from you, because she is wants to find an easy way. That's one of her difficulties. She wants to find an easy way, to quickly grow up. She likes to have a chauffeur drive her. She's a spoilt rich girl really and likes things to be provided for her. She would like you to be on tap for whenever she needs you. I don't think it's such a good idea giving her two sessions on the same day. It's too indulgent.

Participant: But she lives more than a hundred kilometres from the consulting rooms.

DM: She has a chauffeur to drive her. I don't feel too sorry for her really. She's having four sessions a week.

Participant: Is this your idea as a general rule, or just in relation to this patient?

DM: I have, occasionally, because of one thing or another, given a patient two sessions in a day, and I have never found it particularly useful because the patient doesn't go to sleep and dream between the sessions. I think it also can be felt as terribly indulgent and encourage the feeling that you need her rather than that she needs you, or to think that you need the money.

MM: The problem is that the patient is a candidate for training, so she is obliged to have four sessions a week.

DM: She has the makings of a psychoanalyst. She has the imagination. But I shouldn't let the training committee run the analysis. You do your best. You shouldn't let the bureaucracy run the analysis. You'll come to that when the time comes to end her analysis, when she may still be in training, and the training committee will raise hell about it.

MM: Nowadays, she is able to come to São Paulo three times a week so it would be better if we had three sessions, but it's because of the training.

DM: Tell the training committee that you will see her when it's convenient. She has two children. You can't just run her ragged. If she sleeps three nights in São Paulo, you can have four sessions. She has a flat in São Paulo.

MM: Yes, but she works and she has the baby, and she's a candidate.

DM: You'd better spare her a little bit really. When people come a great distance I see them at the weekend when I can, and they stay over till Monday, and I can certainly see them three times a week. It's very expensive to fly every week. You can't run people into the ground financially.

Participant: It need not be on a regular basis. You see them on Saturday, Sunday and Monday, and then Friday, Saturday, Sunday, changing the schedule for the next week.

DM: It's not really very desirable, analytically, because it leaves a huge gap between Sunday and the next Friday. But there is always a gap. The thing is that the bureaucracy of the training shouldn't interfere with the analytic procedure or impose judgement on the analysis.

We often have a situation where someone comes to analysis because they feel they need analysis. Four years later, they have had a very good analysis and they feel completely well, and they like analysis so much they want to train to be an analyst, and the training committee says, 'No, you have to have another analysis.' And the patient says, 'Go to hell, I'm not going to have another analysis.' And I say to the training committee, 'I'm not just going to go through the motions of a second analysis to please you and your regulations.' It's one of the reasons I abandoned the analytic Society, because of this bureaucratic rigidity that interferes with the analysis. They expect you to make reports on your patients. They can go to hell as far as I'm concerned. I'm not making reports on patients. They can use their own judgement if they want to see the patients and evaluate them. It doesn't matter to me, but they can't expect me to write reports on my patients. I might as well be writing reports on my wife, 'Yes, she was very good in bed tonight!' It's none of their business, really. It's too much of an intrusion on the intimacy of the analytic situation.

Participant: In Ribeirão Preto, in the training analysis, we don't make reports on our patients. Unless perhaps the patient might be a terrorist or a criminal – there is an allowance for special cases.

Final considerations

Brigitte's analysis was discontinued the next year owing to personal problems. During his supervisions of her case, Meltzer gradually from her dreams draws a map of her psychic structure, with its geographical and zonal confusions (see his book *The Psychoanalytical Process*). In this scenario he emphasises her feelings of confusion as welcome, and makes a distinc-tion between being confused and feeling confused – where the patient thinks they have got worse but are actually progressing. Confusion between good and bad occurs, according to Klein, when primary splitting is not properly realised; although this looks rigid, it provides the basis for reintegrating split aspects through development.

Meltzer, building on Klein, has in his writings reviewed the problem of mental pain and of developmental processes in the light of Bion's division of mental life into symbolic and non-symbolic spaces. The creation of symbols as a result of learning from experience, in the face of the impact of the beauty of the object, is different from the manipulation of conventional signs. It comes from introjective identification rather than narcissis-tic forms of identification – projective or adhesive – where the beauty of intimacy is hidden behind social armoury directed at survival in the outside world. It is here that Meltzer thinks Klein was mistaken in supposing the paranoid-schizoid position precedes the depressive position, in the baby: if we think of the catastrophic change represented by birth, the defence is rather of closing perceptual openings and fragmenting the sensuous impact of the object.

In the case of Brigitte, the great erotisation of her object and her zonal confusions made her symbolic development more difficult. In the course of the analysis her values seemed to be changing, but our work was interrupted.